THE MINIATURE PINSCHER

Bobbye Land

Project Team
Editor: Amanda Pisani
Copy Editor: Stephanie Fornino
Design: Stephanie Krautheim
Series Design: Stephanie Krautheim and Mada Design
Series Originator: Dominique De Vito

T.F.H. Publications
President/CEO: Glen S. Axelrod
Executive Vice President: Mark E. Johnson
Publisher: Christopher T. Reggio
Production Manager: Kathy Bontz

T.F.H. Publications, Inc.
One TFH Plaza
Third and Union Avenues
Neptune City, NJ 07753

Printed and bound in China

08 09 10 11 12   3 5 7 9 8 6 4 2

Library of Congress Cataloging-in-Publication Data
Land, Bobbye. The miniature pinscher / Bobbye Land.
p. cm.
Includes index.
ISBN 0-7938-3638-7 (alk. paper)
1. Miniature pinscher. I. Title.
SF429.M56L36 2006

  636.76--dc22   2005023947

This book has been published with the intent to provide accurate and authoritative information in regard to the subject matter within. While every reasonable precaution has been taken in preparation of this book, the author and publisher expressly disclaim responsibility for any errors, omissions, or adverse effects arising from the use or application of the information contained herein. The techniques and suggestions are used at the reader's discretion and are not to be considered a substitute for veterinary care. If you suspect a medical problem consult your veterinarian.

The Leader In Responsible Animal Care For Over 50 Years!®
www.tfh.com

TABLE OF CONTENTS

HISTORY
of the Miniature Pinscher

Watch any Miniature Pinscher ("Min Pin") as he races after a toy or small animal, and you can easily see traces of the tenacious little ratter he was hundreds of years ago. After living with a Miniature Pinscher and enjoying his antics and his intelligence, it's easy to see why so many breeds benefited from crossbreeding with Miniature Pinschers in the last few hundred years.

EVOLUTION OF THE MINIATURE PINSCHER

Unlike many breeds that have detailed records following their progression through history, documentation for the Miniature Pinscher only covers the last 200 or so years. Thus, since we can't state facts based on accurate records, we must rely on speculations, based on personal interpretations of old paintings, sculptures, and literature, to try to place the Miniature Pinscher's true beginnings.

Some of the earliest work that researchers noted that contains images suggestive of a Min Pin includes icons depicting Anubis, an Egyptian god who guarded the temple of dead pharaohs. Considering a Min Pin's royal bearing, it is not farfetched to imagine them guarding kings and pharaohs, even into death.

Jumping ahead many decades, a small, fine-boned, cat-sized red dog with prick ears was used as a model in a painting of a peasant family done in the Renaissance period. Many paintings of the 1800s include dogs who greatly resembled the Min Pins of today, so one must assume that the Min Pin's history does indeed span the centuries.

The Miniature Pinscher was originally a small, cat-sized red dog who resembled the Reh deers of the German forests.

German Origins

Setting aside speculation about the breed's very early history, it is believed that the Miniature Pinscher evolved from the ancient German Pinscher family of dogs. This family ultimately produced a number of the breeds recognized by the American Kennel Club (AKC) today, such as the Affenpinscher and the Schnauzers.

Dr. H. G. Reinchenbach, a German writer, is quoted (in writings dated 1836) as saying that the Miniature Pinscher is a cross of the Dachshund and the Italian Greyhound. Historians and those who have researched the background of the breed now generally accept Dr. Reinchenbach's conclusion. Whatever the case, and whatever breeds were used to develop the dog as we know him today, Germany is undisputed as the home of origin of the Min Pin. There, he was known as the "Reh Pinscher" due to his resemblance to a small red deer, the Reh, that freely roamed German forests many years ago.

The Miniature Pinscher is part of the larger German Pinscher family, which contained both large and small varieties. Efforts began to define and distinguish the varieties in the mid-1800s, when breeders no longer crossbred the different coat types. With the formation of the German Pinscher-Schnauzer Klub (PSK) in 1895, there was a concerted effort to combine forces with other pinscher breeders and fanciers to promote and advance the distinct pinscher varieties.

Min Pins at Work

The early Min Pins were considered valuable farm hands because, thanks to their small size and curious nature, they were able to access areas that other animals could not, ridding barnyards and houses of vermin.

Selective Crossbreeding

During the late 1800s, breeders began what appeared to be a mad race to produce the world's tiniest pinscher. In the minds of most people today, this was a drastic and very unfortunate turn of events. For a while, until a trend began toward breeding a sounder animal, the Miniature Pinscher seemed destined for a gene pool riddled with lame, bug-eyed, miniscule canines.

Luckily, people began selective crossbreeding of the German Pinscher, the Dachshund, and the Italian Greyhound, and the Min Pin who emerged has remained largely the same from that time forward. The Min Pin genes today still maintain the traits and qualities of those three original breeds: from the German Pinscher he inherited his terrier-like qualities, including its energy and prey instincts; from the Dachshund, he inherited courage and playful feistiness; and from the Italian Greyhound, he inherited that charming high-stepping, nimble "hackney" gait.

Careful and consistent breeding led to the establishment of the look of today's Miniature Pinscher.

Four Varieties of Pinschers

Bernard Wolphofer's book, *Buch von don Hundon* (*The Book of don Hundon*), describes four varieties of Pinschers existing at the time of writing (1895). These include the Roughhaired German Pinscher, the Roughhaired Dwarf Pinscher, the Smoothhaired German Pinscher, and the Shorthaired Dwarf Pinscher. Although he is a miniature instead of a dwarf, we must assume that the last reference is to the Miniature Pinscher.

To further the notion that at least four kinds of pinschers were common to Germany at about this same time, another book, published in 1897, (Bylandt's *Les Races des Chiens* or *Races of the Dogs*) says that "German dwarf terriers with rough hair conform to the German terrier with smooth hair, and so does the German dwarf terrier with smooth hair." These breeds were obviously well established in German pedigrees.

The Modern German Min Pin

Although the rest of the world had yet to be introduced to the breed at this time, Miniature Pinschers continued to gain in popularity in

Germany through the end of the 1800s, and they became known as exceptional ratters. By the time the new century was well underway, Min Pins were the undisputed "dog du jour" there. Although interest was shown in the breed after its first exhibition at the Stuttgart Dog Show in 1900, it was not extensively bred outside Germany, except in Scandinavian countries, until after 1918.

Obviously, the Miniature Pinscher is still considered a working dog and not a companion animal in Germany. There, he is included in the Guard Dog Group 2 in Germany's FCI classification, along with breeds such as the Great Dane, Mastiff, Rottweiler, and Boxer. This is very different from the US and Canadian Kennel Clubs, which classify the Min Pin as a toy breed. The German Kennel Club still refers to stag red Min Pins as "Reh Pinschers."

MIN PINS IN THE US

According to records, the Min Pin was first imported into the United States in 1919, but none were registered with the American Kennel Club (AKC) until 1925. The first dog was registered as a Pinscher (Toy), and for the next few years, very few were seen at AKC events. When they did finally begin making an appearance at

Mini Dobermans?

Many people mistakenly refer to a Miniature Pinscher as a "Miniature Doberman." However, the Miniature Pinscher was a well-established breed when Louis Dobermann bred his first Doberman Pinscher in 1890. The Miniature Pinscher was obviously in Dobermann's mind, however, when he planned his new breed. He is quoted as saying that he wished to create a breed that he described as "a giant terrier that would look much like the five-pound Reh Pinscher [or Miniature Pinscher as we know him today] but that would be fifteen times heavier and larger." Although his finished breed does somewhat resemble the Miniature Pinscher (particularly in coloring, in which they are nearly identical), it lacks the head type, the classic Min Pin hackneyed gait, and body type.

Part of the confusion about the relationship between the Min Pin and the Doberman likely stems from the fact that the word "pinscher" is found in both names. The word "pinscher," however, is a descriptive term like "setter" or "terrier" that denotes the dog's method of working. "Pinscher" refers to a dog's habit of jumping on and fiercely biting his quarry, something the Min Pin became adept at when doing his original job of ridding homes and farms of rats. It is also worth noting that a definition in *Henne's Dictionary of the German Language* indicates that the word "pinscher" is "borrowed from the English word 'pincher,' meaning one who pinches, nips, or tweaks."

The word "pinscher" refers to a habit of jumping on and fiercely biting a prey quarry, a trait that was highly valued by early breeders.

shows, they were shown in the Miscellaneous class and were not given their own individual breed classes. Once the Miniature Pinscher Club of America (MPCA) was formed (in 1929) and a standard was submitted to and approved by the AKC, the Miniature Pinscher was shown in the Terrier Group and began his quick ascent to the top of the popularity charts. In 1930, the breed was moved into the Toy Group, where it is still shown today. It was registered and shown for many years as a "Pinscher (Miniature)," and it was not until 1972 that the breed became officially known as the Miniature Pinscher, or more affectionately, the Min Pin.

The Development of the Breed Standard in the US

The first breed standard written in the United States was published with a courtesy acknowledgment to the Pinscher Schnauzer Clubs of Giesen, Germany. This standard made reference to the Min Pin being "similar in appearance to the Doberman Pinscher." In 1935, a revised standard made an even stronger reference to the Doberman by stating that the Min Pin should be considered "a miniature of the Doberman Pinscher." That same year, in a column for the *AKC Gazette*, Helen Coster reported the response to her inquiry to the German Kennel Club in Stuttgart regarding the early beginnings of the Miniature Pinscher. According to their letter of reply, "the Zwerg or Dwarf Pinscher is a pure German breed from olden times, and…it has nothing to do with the Doberman or the Manchester Terrier." By the time the standard was completely revised in 1950 and historical proof had been gathered as to the Min Pin's heritage, all references to the Doberman were eliminated. The standard was revised again in 1958 and again in 1980. Although many changes to the breed standard have occurred (such as the shape of head, eyes, and general conformation), the breed's innate character, regal bearing, childish intent to get into mischief, and fierce loyalty and devotion to family have never faltered or been changed.

BREED CLUBS

Every pure breed of dog in the United States has a parent club that is responsible for making decisions in the breed's best interests. The parent club determines and monitors issues as to registration, titles, and the breed standard, and it finds answers to any questions that arise concerning its chosen breed.

The Miniature Pinscher Club of America was formed and recognized by the AKC in 1929. Additionally, there are 13 "local" Miniature Pinscher Clubs spread throughout the United States. The MPCA holds an annual Specialty Show between March 1 and June 30 of each year, with a rotating location throughout the country. This annual Specialty Show has become a two-day event and

Today, the beloved Miniature Pinscher is one of the most popular breeds in the world.

The clubs of people that form around particular breeds help support and care for the well-being of the breed.

includes puppy sweepstakes, regular conformation showing, and obedience competition. Each member of MPCA receives the club's official publication, *The Pinscher Patter*, which is mailed quarterly and which provides a wealth of information on the breed.

The MPCA requires each applicant to sign a detailed code of ethics that describes exactly what is expected of any person who is accepted as a member. This code mandates that members not only give ethical treatment to all dogs in their care, but that they act responsibly toward any Min Pin who appears in need of aid. Members must agree to conduct their puppy sales in a responsible manner and to accept responsibility for every puppy they produce throughout the dog's entire life.

It is because of the hard work of MPCA officers

Celebrity Min Pins

Although the people who love them believe Min Pins to be the dog world's best-kept secret, the secret is out among a few select celebrities. Mamie Van Doren (bombshell of the B-movie drive-in era) is proudly owned by a fiesty chocolate Min Pin named "Starlett," and Joey Fatone (of the group *NSYNC) proudly holds aloft his Min Pin "Nikita" during a group photo shoot.

and members that genetic testing, designed to ultimately bring an end to genetic health problems, is available. Club leaders make strong suggestions and recommendations about the guidelines their members should follow when making decisions for their individual breeding programs, and they always urge members to breed only when they will be bettering the breed for future generations. Breed clubs, such as the MPCA and its parent club, the AKC, are committed to bringing about a greater understanding of the purebred dog and his role in society. Every Min Pin owner is urged to get involved with one or more breed clubs and to help maintain the clubs' core objective by being a responsible pet owner and by ensuring that her Min Pin is a well-mannered, well-trained, and responsible member of society—a good ambassador for all purebred dogs.

The American Kennel Club

The mission statement of the American Kennel Club provides that as a registry of purebred dogs, its goal is to preserve the integrity of that registry. AKC-sanctioned dog events promote interest in and sustain the process of breeding for type and function of purebred dogs. Does registration by the AKC guarantee any

Members of the Miniature Pinscher Club of America have the objective of promoting quality in the responsible breeding of purebred Min Pins.

dog's health or quality? Absolutely not. It is only a recording organization. Although the AKC records the parentage of over a million dogs annually, it states firmly that any purebred dog who is registered with it should never be considered as having a "seal of approval." The club promotes public education in choosing the proper breed of dog and how to choose a responsible breeder.

It takes years of dedication and involvement to recognize the best qualities of a purebred Min Pin.

In its quest to unite the dog-buying public with the perfect purebred dog for their family, the AKC supports numerous programs to educate the general public about the proper way to find a reputable breeder and assess which breed and which puppy is best suited to the buyer's needs and lifestyle.

The Kennel Club

The Kennel Club's primary objective is to promote, in every way, the general improvement of dogs.

This objective is to be achieved through:

- Ensuring that the Kennel Club is the first port of call on all canine matters.
- Recognizing the importance of canine health and welfare.
- Popularizing canine events, with a focus on the retention of existing customers and the attraction of new.
- Achieving a widening of the Kennel Club membership base.
- Encouraging the development of all those concerned with dogs through education and training.
- Encouraging more people to provide input into the Kennel Club's decision-making process.

Chapter 2

CHARACTERISTICS
of the Miniature Pinscher

It only takes one look at the twinkle in a Miniature Pinscher's eye to know that in human equivalents he would be the class clown of any group. Retaining his "perpetual puppyhood" well into middle age and even the geriatric stage, the Min Pin makes a wonderful pet for almost any situation. While not well suited for very young children (who could easily cause them great harm), Min Pins will adapt well to almost any family or lifestyle. Their temperament is so much a part of what distinguishes a Min Pin from any other breed that the parent club described this delightful animal as featuring "fearless animation, complete self-possession, and spirited presence."

A STANDARD OF EXCELLENCE

The breed standard describes a dog of "balance." From his well-balanced head, with no extremes of angle, to his body, the Min Pin is a balanced little dog. He is short-coupled and compact and has the movement of a well-trained athlete. His hackney-like gait is unique, and combined with his spirited presence in the ring, makes for a good example of the breed. He is a consummate show dog. Fearless and attention seeking, he seems to believe that each round of applause for the dogs who precede and follow him are instead aimed at him. He is easily groomed and seems filled with pride at his appearance.

With this image in mind, let's go point by point throughout the breed standard and see what it really describes. After all, how else would you know the perfect Miniature Pinscher if you saw him?

The Min Pin Head

Let's take it from the top and start with the head. Breeders try very hard to keep a Min Pin's head in correct proportion to the rest of his body. The dog's head should always appear smooth, never coarse or heavy. It should be elongated and not rounded or "apple domed."

The eyes should never be round but rather appear slightly oval.

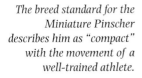

The breed standard for the Miniature Pinscher describes him as "compact" with the movement of a well-trained athlete.

What Is a Standard?

A standard is a written description of the ideal dog in any pure breed. A dog's standard is approved first by the breed's parent club and then by the national kennel club. It describes the characteristics that distinguish one breed from another.

The present AKC standard for Miniature Pinschers was submitted by the Miniature Pinscher Club of America and accepted by the American Kennel Club on July 8, 1980. (The standard was reformatted on February 21, 1990.) The present standard for Miniature Pinschers in Great Britain was accepted by that country's national Kennel Club in July of 2001.

Eyes (and eye rims) should be so dark as to appear black, although a lighter eye and eye rim is accepted in dogs with coats of chocolate or blue. People who share their lives with a Min Pin believe that the standard should call for eyes with a mischievous sparkle or glint, as this quality does seem to be a trademark of the breed.

The ears are one of the first things one notices about a Min Pin, as they are expressive and set high, standing erect from base to tip. Most owners have their Min Pin's ears cropped, but more and more are being left uncropped.

The skull appears flat, tapering forward toward the muzzle, which should be strong rather than fine and delicate, and in proportion to the head as a whole. There should be no appearance of loose skin or wrinkles on the face and muzzle.

The nose should always be black, unless the dog is of a chocolate color. Chocolate Min Pins should have a self-colored (chocolate-colored) nose.

The Min Pin has a gracefully curved neck, and his facial features include expressive ears, teeth that meet in a scissors bite, and eyes that sparkle.

A Min Pin's teeth should always meet in a scissors bite.

The Min Pin's head is set on a slightly arched neck that is proportioned in size to head and body. The gracefully curved neck, blending smoothly into the shoulders, should appear muscled but not bulky and should be free from any excess skin.

Size Matters

Size does matter—when you're a Min Pin at least. Any Min Pin who is under 10 inches (25.4 cm) or over 12.5 inches (31.8 cm) in height will be disqualified from the show ring and should usually not be considered a part of any breeding program.

The Perfect Physique

A Min Pin body is compact and sturdy, his muscles well defined but not overdone. His forechest should be well developed, not sunken, and he should have well-sprung ribs, without appearing barrel-chested. His belly should be neatly tucked up to exude an air of gracefulness. The brisket (chest) should be no deeper than level with the points of the elbows. His tail should be set on his body in a line that continues his topline (the line running from the dog's shoulders to his tail set). It is held erect and proudly and should be docked in proportion to the size of the dog.

Movement and Legs

Some people refer to the Min Pin as the "pony dog," and indeed, he does have many characteristics of a gaited horse. His curved neck and graceful carriage, with head and tail carried high, is much like that of an Arabian horse, and his gait resembles that of a

A Miniature Pinscher moves with a distinct gait that has been likened to an Arabian horse.

Tennessee Walker with his high-prancing style. The forelegs and hind legs move parallel, with feet turning neither in nor out. This action is a high-stepping, free and easy gait in which the front leg moves straight forward and in front of the body, and the foot bends at the wrist. The dog drives smoothly and strongly from the rear.

Like a good horse, the Min Pin should show no evidence of a sway (dipped) or roached

The coloration of Min Pins is important, and one of the most common combinations is black with rust markings.

(humped) back, and he should carry his topline level or slightly sloping toward the rear both when he is moving and standing still.

The Min Pin's correct movement is that of a hackney pony, and it should never be a sloppy movement. To maintain this precision gait, the shoulders must be clean (running smoothly down the dog's neck past the shoulder blades) and sloping with moderate angulation to allow the hackney action while still keeping elbows close to the body. The legs must be strong and sturdy, although they appear fragile.

The feet of a proper Min Pin actually look more like cat feet than those of a dog. Dewclaws (extra, unused nails that usually occur on the lower portion of the front legs) should be removed to maintain the clean, elegant line of the leg.

A Min Pin's thighs should be well muscled and set widely apart to fit smoothly into a body that has a perfect overall balance. When standing or moving, he should never appear cow hocked (with the toes facing outward) when viewed from the rear.

Coat and Color

The coat of a Min Pin should be smooth, hard, and short, and it should lie tightly against the body. Coloration is important on the Min Pin. A dog in compliance with the breed standard may be solid clear red, stag red, black, or chocolate. No other colors are acceptable for conformation classes, although Min Pins of any color can compete in other AKC events. A stag red color is red with the intermingling of a few black hairs, and in both clear and stag red, a rich, deep color is preferred over a lighter red. Another acceptable black coloration is black with rust-red markings on the cheeks, lips, lower jaw, throat, eyebrows, chest, the lower half of the forelegs, inside of the hind legs and beneath the tail, and the lower portion of the hocks and feet on the rear legs, with black "pencil stripes" on the toes. A chocolate-colored Min Pin will have the same rust-red markings in the same places as on the blacks but feature chocolate pencil striping rather than black striping on the toes.

The color of a Min Pin is considered to be very important. (Be aware that some unscrupulous breeders will try to sell "blue" Min Pins, under the guise that this is a special, "rare" color. A blue coloration is undesirable and you should steer clear.) It is also a disqualification to have a "thumb mark" on the front of the foreleg—this mark is inside the rust markings and is black on black dogs and chocolate in chocolate dogs. It is also a disqualification to

"Rare" Min Pins

Don't be lured into purchasing a Miniature Pinscher who does not fit the breed standard simply because he is advertised as "rare." Once in a while you'll see someone advertise a "blue" or "fawn" Min Pin or one who is not within the size allowance, sometimes with an exaggerated price tag. "Blue" (actually blue-gray) is a disqualification in the show ring. Being "unusual" or "rare" does not make a dog worth more; in fact, the price should be lower, because "blue" Min Pins have been linked with alcopecia (hair loss) and a poor, thin coat, as well as other more severe skin conditions.

A blue-eyed Min Pin is not considered acceptable by the Miniature Pinscher Club of America according to its breed standard. The standard calls for brown eyes, and although a dog who has a "blue" coat or eyes will be as special a pet as any other Min Pin, he should not be considered "desirable" and certainly should *never* be considered as part of a breeding program.

The Miniature Pinscher, the "King of Toys," is outgoing, assertive, spirited, and independent. He is a lot of dog in a little body.

have white on any part of the dog that exceeds ½ inch (1.3 cm) in any direction.

MIN PIN CHARACTER

Often referred to as "The King of Toys" this proud little dog with such royal bearing is a self-assured, exuberant, and lively dog with, as the breed standard states, "fearless animation, complete self-possession, and spirited presence." However, he plays the part of the clown so easily that some say he's more appropriately deemed the "Court Jester" than the "King." The Miniature Pinscher fears nothing, which can get him into a lot of trouble (not the least of which is finding himself alone and far from home after making a mad dash after an interesting prey). Because Min Pins were originally bred as ratters, anything that moves quickly is considered fair game for them, no matter the size.

Miniature Pinschers are truly a lot of bang in a little firework. Measuring only 10 inches (25.4 cm) to 12.5 inches (31.8 cm) at the shoulder, these charming little dynamos can alter your world—both physically and emotionally. They are the ultimate companion dog, loving and loyal, but don't underestimate their passionate desire to have their own way, a trait that makes housetraining, obedience work, and safe confinement a challenge in dog ownership.

"Pinsch"

The Miniature Pinscher originated in Germany, where he was used to hunt rats and vermin. The word "pinsch" is German for "grab" or "snatch." Most Min Pins today retain that instinct and will chase and grab anything that moves quickly, shaking it soundly until it stops moving.

Many people wrongfully refer to Min Pins as "miniature Dobermans." Although they appear alike at first glance, Miniature Pinschers certainly bear little resemblance to Doberman Pinschers, who have a more serious attitude toward life. They are intensely curious, which can get them into trouble in a dozen different ways on any given day, and they are always full of vigor, which can make them difficult for the average person to keep up with.

LOCATION, LOCATION, LOCATION

One great quality of the Miniature Pinscher is that he is a great pet for any type of environment. Min Pins are good dogs for city living, the suburban home, or the farm. As long as they receive plenty of exercise, they are happy wherever their owners are.

The Great Outdoors

When he's outside, you will always have to be very careful with your Min Pin. If he's allowed out of doors off lead, his high prey drive may kick in at the sight of a passing squirrel or floating leaf. He might also just take off for the joy of having you chase *him.* You should also make sure to dog-proof your yard so that your Min Pin can't get into trouble. (And you'll find that with a Min Pin, even a minute can be long enough for him to get into trouble.) Fences must be strong and flawless. If you find a hole, you can bet that your Min Pin can find it as well. Once he's found it, he'll be through it and halfway to the next county before you even realize he's missing. And just because you didn't find an escape route today doesn't mean that he won't find one (or create his own) tomorrow. Owning a Min Pin means staying on your toes and keeping one step ahead of his active imagination and curious mind.

In the Home

Because of the Min Pin's natural tendency to be curious about and investigate everything, it is absolutely essential for his safety that protective measures be taken when safety-proofing his home. Never leave small objects (such as coins, medicine, paper clips, pens, and cigarette butts) lying around, even where you think your Min Pin can't reach them. Keep electric cords encased or out of reach, as dogs often will chew on them and suffer the consequences.

Like owning any dog, having a Min Pin in the house will serve as a good lesson in tidiness. If you have a fondness for a particular pair of shoes, I suggest that you put them in the closet and shut the door well. Items left on the floor are up for grabs—no dog can distinguish your new designer footwear from a chew toy.

SOCIAL SKILLS

As with all dogs, socializing is very important. Min Pins are not a breed that does well when left alone. They need people, and they should be comfortable enough with people to get the companionship that they crave.

Min Pins and Adults

Min Pins are one of the few breeds that can be happy with

Min Pins are curious and love to explore. If let off lead in an unsecured area, they may quickly take off after something and be difficult to find.

almost any home situation. They are active enough to fit into an active adult home or one with older children, and they are equally happy to be lap warmers for elderly folks. They're well known for their desire to snuggle deep under the covers and "hibernate" with their humans. In fact, they will thrive in almost any situation where they are allowed to be with their humans. A Min Pin who is not properly socialized can easily become jumpy and jittery around people, which can lead to a host of other problems.

Kids and Min Pins

It is important for children to realize that even as a full-grown adult, the Miniature Pinscher is still going to be a very small dog. He is fearless and may oftentimes jump from heights that will astound you, landing on his feet like a cat and none the worse for wear. However, being dropped from even the height of a child's arms can do serious injury to your pet.

It is impossible to answer the question "Are Miniature Pinschers

This Miniature Pinscher is comfortable around birds, and while the breed generally gets along well with just about everyone, it is best to make introductions carefully.

good with children?" without first answering the question "Are the children in question good with dogs?" Children should be taught how to interact with animals, especially dogs, long before you consider adopting a dog as a pet. Children and dogs left alone together are an accident waiting to happen, and it is worth noting that

With clear instructions and gentle but firm training, your Min Pin will soon learn manners and house rules.

dog bites seldom occur when a parent or guardian supervises their interaction. No dog should be expected to continually take abuse at the hands of any human, no matter how small those hands. Problems between dogs and children are usually easily preventable with responsible dog training and responsible parenting.

Children too young to know better can chase, scream at, grab, or yank at a dog's tail or ears. Min Pins will not endure this behavior, and a bite may follow. A Min Pin who does not love children was most probably raised in a household that allowed the children to grab him and treat him roughly without intervention from a responsible adult.

Lizards and Tomcats and Birds— Oh My!

The Miniature Pinscher, if socialized and trained properly, can be great with other dogs and pets, although it's not advisable to leave them alone with smaller animals (such as hamsters and rabbits) that they can consider prey. With other dogs, they tend to try to be the dominant alpha dog in the pack, so you should feel certain that other dogs in

Challenges of Min Pin Ownership

Despite their ability to worm their way into even the hardest heart, these wonderful little dogs often find their way into rescue situations, including humane societies and city shelters. How can this be?

Many times dogs in shelters have an owner somewhere who is desperately searching for them. Min Pins are excellent escape artists, and they should not be allowed out of doors unsupervised, even if in a securely fenced area, and absolutely never off lead. Sadly, many beloved Min Pins never find their original owners (a great reason for your Min Pin to be microchipped and/or tattooed).

In addition, the Miniature Pinscher is not the easiest dog to housetrain, and some owners just give up. It takes great consistency to housetrain a Min Pin. Other people find that they're experiencing a conflict between their Min Pin and their new baby. While a Min Pin doesn't have a vicious bone in his body, he can be very jealous of an "intrusive" newcomer such as an infant. This is why it's extremely important to use proper socialization techniques when you're planning to add any other living creature to your household, whether it's another pet or a human baby.

Min Pins can be barkers, and some can be destructive, behaviors that may prove too much for a new dog owner to take. Min Pins are a lot of action in a tiny body, and if they're not given proper exercise and enough "work" to do, you can expect them to take out their boredom on your belongings. You can also expect them to use their vocal chords to tell anyone who'll listen about their displeasure with the given situation.

Of course, I'm a firm believer that the advantages of owning a Min Pin far outweigh the possible downsides, but it's important to know that these little dogs do present challenges to some owners.

the family will be tolerant of your Min Pin's "Napoleon Syndrome." In fact, you should always watch your Min Pin around large dogs. It's not likely that the larger dog will hurt your Min Pin by stepping on him, but rather that your little pet will overstep his bounds and try to put the big guy in his place!

Neutering your pet is one of the most important keys to having a dog-friendly animal, and it can certainly make things run more smoothly in your family "pack."

ARE MIN PINS EASY TO TRAIN?

Training a Min Pin requires you to know a lot more than he

does. You may know more about geography and history, but the typical Min Pin has a brain that works at warp speed at all times and can figure out the answer to a perplexing problem (such as how to get that crumb from beneath the refrigerator) in record time. Generally, the Min Pin is a pretty stubborn guy, and it may take a while for you to get your ideas across to him, but he inherently wants to please. These dogs are not slow learners; instead, they are independent thinkers — once they've "got it," they remember it. They seem to have limitless energy, which also makes them an excellent choice for a performance dog.

Because of their effervescent character, it takes a special person to enjoy training and showing a Min Pin. Depending on their mood on any particular day, Min Pins can leave the crowd in awe of their prowess and intelligence, but equally as often, they can leave onlookers laughing out loud at their antics. In fact, owners and trainers of Min Pins quickly learn that a good sense of humor is imperative when trying to work with one of these little half-pint jesters.The more someone laughs at them, the harder they will try to earn more laughs. However, when they settle into a serious moment in the obedience ring, few other breeds can top them, and many have earned the highest obedience and agility ratings and titles possible.

Want to know more about Miniature Pinschers? You should ask as many questions as possible of people who know the breed best before you decide to share your home with one. It's certainly not the perfect breed for everyone, but for those who make the commitment to love and share their space with one, there can be no more perfect dog.

Miniature Pinschers are very intelligent dogs.

27

PREPARING
for Your Miniature Pinscher

B ringing a Min Pin home to share your life and be part of your family is a major decision. Certainly it's one that requires a lot of homework and dedicated discussion with all family members. Before you purchased your last vehicle, you probably gathered as much information as possible regarding its safety record, fuel needs, maintenance requirements, and daily operational requirements. Doesn't acquiring a new family member who will be with you for a lifetime deserve more consideration than picking out a machine that will serve you for only a few years before it is replaced?

BEFORE YOU BUY A DOG

Before you decide to get any dog, but especially a Min Pin, you should first discuss the decision thoroughly with every member of the family—remembering that the opinion of everyone must be carefully considered, as every member of the household will have certain expectations in connection with the dog. Remember, too, that each person will be responsible for at least some part of the dog's care and training. Choosing a Min Pin for the right reasons makes it more likely that he will become a valued member of your home. Choosing one for the wrong reasons can be disastrous for you both. Shelters and rescue facilities are filled with Miniature Pinschers who have no fault other than that the wrong family, for the wrong reasons, chose them.

Take the time to fully understand the kind of dog a Min Pin is before bringing him into your family.

Before you bring home a Min Pin, remember that there are advantages and disadvantages to caring for a dog. Playing ball in the park with your Min Pin on a sunny day will be fun. Walking him in the rain and scooping his poop will not. However, these are all very real activities for dog owners. Admittedly, most reputable breeders will take back any Min Pin who does not work out in his new situation, but it's not fair to the dog to shuffle him around from home to home when his only fault is being a normal Miniature Pinscher. Be aware that if you've purchased your puppy from someone who does not offer any help if it doesn't work out, you may be faced with turning him over to a shelter, where his chances of being adopted will be very slim.

Don't take chances with a Min Pin's life. Make certain this is what you want and that you're willing to do whatever it takes to make it work. Your Min Pin will be the one to ultimately pay the price for a hasty, impulse-driven decision.

Min Pin Pros and Cons

There is no perfect breed. All dogs have issues concerning genetic health, temperament, daily care needs, or specific training needs, and Min Pins are no exception. As a result, if anyone tries to sell you a Min Pin without explaining the challenges of owning one, run fast and far. This person doesn't have your best interests at heart, and she certainly doesn't have her breed's best interests at heart, either!

Min Pins are definitely not a breed for everyone, and those who love them the most will be the first to say so. They can be high maintenance with respect to their need for lots of activity, and their innate stubbornness means that they may require more stringent

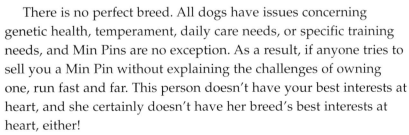

training practices when housetraining and learning basic manners. But if they have been bred carefully and are raised properly, they are basically a healthy breed with good temperaments. Those who share their lives with a Min Pin firmly believe that there is no other breed as far as they are concerned!

Once you've weighed the pros and cons of owning a Min Pin and are confident in your choice, your search for the perfect Min Pin for you can begin. Patience is the key to a happy relationship with your future dog. Don't be swayed by a cute face and bright eyes. This is a long-term commitment that shouldn't be rushed into on an impulse.

Why Do You Really Want a Dog?

I advise people to really search their hearts about why they want a dog in their lives. Some of the reasons that people want a dog seem obvious and rational, but upon closer inspection, they don't always hold up.

Before you decide to get a Min Pin, give the matter a lot of thought before making your final decision.

A Dog for the Kids

If you want to get a dog "for the children," you should give the matter a lot more thought before making your final decision. It may seem obvious that children benefit from growing up with a four-footed best friend, but just as with any new toy, once the "new" has worn off the situation, the daily care of your Min Pin will undoubtedly end up being the responsibility of an adult. Be sure that *you* want a dog and that *you* are willing and ready to take on the extra time and effort necessary to raise an active Min Pin.

Watch Dog

Looking for a dog to guard the house? Admittedly, most Min Pins have a healthy bark (that they seem to love to hear), and most can readily go into defense mode when their family is threatened, but let's be honest here—their size will keep them from

These little darlings will soon grow into Min Pin pistols, ready to take on the world. Will you be ready for them?

serving as a deterrent to a determined burglar. An alarm system, security fence, or any of a dozen other measures will be far less expensive in the long run than adopting a canine burglar alarm.

Got a Good Deal

Have you ever heard the saying "You get what you pay for?" A "bargain" Min Pin is probably no bargain and may cost you significantly more in veterinary bills, training, and other expenses than an appropriately priced pet. Choosing a family member to share your life is definitely *not* the time to cut corners.

Earn Extra Income as a Breeder

If you think that you'll make money breeding puppies, you really *do* need to do your homework! Besides the fact that shelters are overcrowded with purebreds (yes, even Min Pins) and mixed breeds and there are simply not enough good permanent homes for them all, there's the simple fact that done *correctly* (with both practical and academic knowledge under your belt), breeding any breed of dog is often a money-losing proposition. Moreover, because Min Pins have small litters with a great possibility of whelping complications (meaning you stand a good chance of losing your pet while she is birthing puppies), the puppies you might produce most likely wouldn't be worth the effort from a monetary point of view. (Note: You should certainly visit a shelter and look into the faces of all the homeless dogs, as well as go to the many Min Pin Rescue websites and see the wonderful dogs available there, before you consider breeding even one litter of puppies.)

Min Pins Are so Cute!

Some of the absolute worst reasons to choose a breed of dog are because of its physical appearance or its popularity. Often, movies and television shows star rare or unique breeds that are unsuitable for most normal family situations. Min Pins are certainly no different. While their perky appearance makes them a natural for advertisements and entertainment, they are definitely not a breed for everyone.

A Dog to Truly Love

If you want to share your home with a canine companion and you're willing to wait until the right puppy or adult comes along, I encourage you to proceed. This is the only acceptable reason to make the decision to open your home to any dog, especially a Min Pin. Everyone may have different activities they want to share with their Min Pin, from showing in conformation to competing in performance events such as agility, flyball, or obedience, but the main reason to buy a dog should be because you want a pet to share your home.

Your Lifestyle

A Min Pin is adaptable to almost any type of living arrangements provided that he has adequate room for exercise. As you consider whether to get a dog, bear in mind that he will be happiest in a home where someone is home with him during the day, preferably in a place with a secure fenced area to occasionally romp and play on his own. Unless you can make a firm commitment to always walk him on leash when he is outdoors, even when you're sick and the weather is bad, a fenced yard is a must for any Min Pin. Because this breed was originally bred to track and kill small prey, its intense need to chase its quarry—

Cost and Effect

Living with a Min Pin (or any other breed) is not cheap. Most carry a significant price tag, and their food, supplies, and normal medical care expenses can easily add up to quite a bit of money each year. If you plan to groom your own dog, you'll have to purchase the tools to do so. Granted, these are far less expensive than tools for grooming a long-haired dog, but it still adds up. When you factor in the possibility of accidents and unexpected illnesses, it's apparent that adding a Min Pin to your family will require you to devote a fairly large chunk of the family budget to your dog.

Your Min Pin will not let you forget that he wants and needs you. Your relationship will flourish if you have the time, patience, and devotion for this breed.

combined with an inquisitive nature—makes it impossible for a Min Pin to be allowed out into the world on his own without supervision. A Min Pin who is allowed off leash is a Min Pin who will likely be seen on "Lost Dog" posters around the neighborhood.

Ready for the Min Pin Plunge?

So, have you decided yet? Are you sure you're ready to share your heart and home with a dog? Have you decided whether you are indeed a Min Pin person? Let's see how you honestly answer the following questions:

- Can you find the time every single day to take your Min Pin for walks, as well as find time for trips to the veterinarian and to groom and bathe him when necessary?
- Is your entire family committed to spending the next 10 to 14 years providing health care, food, grooming, training, and love for a family pet?
- Will you ensure that your children strictly follow the "house rules" you've set for your Min Pin? Will you be willing to teach your children (and enforce your guidelines to the letter) to respect your Min Pin's space, as well as teach them to handle and treat the dog properly?
- Do you think you'll make a good dog person? A good Min Pin person? Are you patient? Flexible? Loving and nurturing? Are you a neat freak who wants everything in its place both inside and outside your home? Would dog hair or drool (or possibly worse) on the furniture be considered a major problem?
- Major changes in your life, such as having a baby, caring for elderly parents, divorcing, and taking a new job or losing your job are all things that might alter your ability to care for a pet.

Are any of these changes possibilities in your near future? If these things came up unexpectedly, could taking care of your Min Pin be a top priority?

- Are you physically, financially, and emotionally able to care for an active, adventure-seeing Miniature Pinscher on a day-to-day basis?

- Is your home environment prepared to adequately accommodate a Min Pin? If not, are you willing to make the investment of time and money necessary to ensure that it is? Is your yard, or a portion of it, securely fenced? Or are you willing to spend time each day making sure that your Min Pin gets adequate supervised exercise?

- Can you or another family member make time to be home at least part of the day for a while until your Min Pin is settled into his new situation?

- Do you have the time, patience, and inclination to train a Min Pin puppy? If the answer is no, would you consider adopting an older dog instead of a puppy?

- Do you enjoy meeting new people? It's a given that taking a walk with your Min Pin will bring attention to both you and your pet, and passersby will inevitably stop you to chat about their experiences with Min Pins.

- Last but most importantly, are you ready to share your home with an ebullient, bursting-with-energy, tiny clown who will find or create humor in any situation—one who will love you with an astounding devotion, no matter whether you deserve it or not and fill a hole in your life that you weren't aware was even there?

If you answered these

You'll know you've made the right choice to welcome a Min Pin into your life when you see a face like this one looking up at you.

questions positively, then *yes*, you're undoubtedly going to make an excellent "Min Pin person."

Puppy or Adult?

Whew! The hardest part is over, right? The decision has been made—you definitely want to be a Min Pin family. Ah, but that's just the first in a long line of decisions yet to be made. The next one in line is whether you want a puppy or an adult dog.

A Pinscher Pup

There is certainly nothing cuter in the world than a Min Pin puppy. With his bright eyes, cheeky, innocent grin, and perky ebullience, he charms the heart of everyone he meets. But having your heart charmed and being realistic about what your family needs, wants, *and* can realistically manage are two different things.

If you're a parent, you remember how much a human baby changes a routine. Well, a puppy is going to need very much the same level of attention and time spent on him as a human baby.

Older Min Pins make excellent pets for people who don't have the energy for a young puppy.

And although he won't be a baby for quite as long as a human, he will still have special needs long enough to disrupt your schedule.

He will have to be watched and entertained at all times to keep him out of trouble. He will also need to be fed four times a day and taken outside to potty every three to four hours. You'll also need to schedule time for your Min Pin's regular veterinary visits every few weeks until he's several months old.

An Adult Dog

If you're not quite ready for the responsibility and time involved in raising a puppy, it sounds as though you'd be a good candidate for adopting a rescue or other pre-owned adult Min Pin.

If you have very small children, an older Min Pin is likely a better choice for your family. (Don't be insulted if a breeder refuses to place a Min Pin of any age with your family if you have young toddlers. Remember, she has to always have her dogs' best interest in mind. Perhaps if you spend time around her and her Min Pins, showing her that your children have been taught how to act around dogs and how to handle them properly, she may change her mind.) A young puppy might be more rambunctious and could harm a small child without meaning to, and certainly young children who have a problem determining between their stuffed animal and the family pet can injure a puppy quite easily.

Senior citizens or physically challenged adults who may not have the energy, physical ability, or desire to keep up with a younger puppy may find that an older pet is an excellent choice for them. There's also a good chance that an older Min Pin has already been housetrained, and even if he's not, it's easier to train an adult than a puppy who seems to have to urinate every 20 minutes. Another plus is that an older Min Pin can be neutered before he comes to you.

Afraid an older Min Pin won't bond with you as well as a younger puppy would? Forget it! Any dog professional will agree that a dog adopted as an oldster appreciates your care and quickly becomes even more devoted—after all, it's likely he knows what it's like to live in a world without love. Besides, the hand that holds a Min Pin's food bowl holds his heart.

Of course, not every adult Min Pin who's looking for a home is going to be perfect for you, any more than every puppy would be. The older Min Pin may have health or temperament challenges that caused him to end up looking for a new home in the first place. Before you consider adopting an older Min Pin, you should find out as much about him as possible. Get a definitive and thorough explanation of any problems. If you don't understand what you're being told, have it explicitly clarified for you. If the dog has health issues, make sure they are easily and inexpensively treatable. If you're not an experienced dog trainer, be wary of any Min Pin who needs specific training for temperament or behavior issues. Above all else, be sure that you are getting this secondhand Min Pin through a reputable source who will be candid with you about his problems.

A Min Pin who habitually bites humans or displays aggressive tendencies should never be brought into a home with small

Take Your Time

Whether you decide to look for a baby Min Pin or you start checking out the rescue pages, remember the following key things:

1. Be sure you're ready for the responsibility of owning a Min Pin.

2. Take your time in the search for the perfect Min Pin for your family. The right dog is out there, just waiting for you to find him and let him love you. He's worth the wait!

children and should be evaluated carefully by a professional to determine whether he is adoptable into *any* home situation. A Min Pin who barks obsessively should not be adopted by someone who is not home for long periods of time throughout the day. The very busy, hyperactive Min Pin should be avoided if you live alone in an apartment and are gone for long periods of time; he needs a home with a large fenced yard and a large family to keep him entertained. No matter how much you want to do a good thing and save a homeless Min Pin's life, some behaviors simply are not acceptable. Be honest with yourself about the severity of any concern and your ability to manage it.

Dogs of all ages become available for adoption for dozens of reasons, many of which are unrelated to the dog himself, so don't think you're settling for second choice by adopting a rescue dog. Reasons that a Min Pin may become available range from the sad (death of an owner), to the uneducated ("he sheds," "he needs too much attention," "he is too expensive"), to the ridiculous ("he no longer matches our home décor," "he isn't cute and cuddly any more," "we want a new puppy"). These unfortunate reasons can create a tragic situation for an innocent Min Pin who only wants to love and be loved. You'll find that giving one of these abandoned Min Pins a new chance at life is very rewarding.

A purebred Miniature Pinscher represents a proud ancestry of all the dogs who have gone before him.

Pet or Show Quality?

The next consideration is what you expect to do with your new pet. Do you want a companion to join you on early morning jogs? Do you want a Min Pin to take with your family to the beach or on fishing trips? Maybe you simply want a Min Pin companion to snuggle with on the couch to watch TV. Do you want to get involved in performance events such as agility, obedience, or tracking? Perhaps you've watched a few dog shows on television or have attended your local kennel club show and decided that showing dogs looks like fun. You must have a firm idea in mind what kind of dog you're looking for before you purchase your Min Pin, because "pet or show quality?" will be one of the first questions you need to answer.

Pet-Quality Puppies

Don't think that by taking a "pet" Min Pin that you're getting a puppy of lesser quality. And don't expect your puppy to be bargain-basement priced because he has some flaw. Sometimes the only difference between a "show" Min Pin and a "pet" Min Pin may be a coloration issue or some other seemingly frivolous point.

The long ear on this Min Pin would certainly limit his chances in the show ring, but it won't make him any less qualified as your devoted companion.

Breeders must be very choosy about what dogs they keep to show. Showing dogs is an expensive sport, and only the best-quality puppies should be kept for exhibition and future breeding plans. These breeders invested a lot of knowledge, time, and money to create those cute little bundles, and even the puppies who are somewhat "less than perfect" for one reason or another have the potential to give you many years of love and companionship. Remember, all dogs are "pets" to someone, even if they go on to enter the Min Pin history books with an illustrious show and breeding career.

If you choose a pet-quality Min Pin, you may be given AKC Limited Registration papers instead of a full AKC registration certificate. This means that although your Min Pin is fully AKC registered, his offspring could not be registered with the club. If your Min Pin was not of sufficient quality for the breeder to keep him to show and possibly breed, she will likely feel that he should not be allowed to reproduce. If a breeder offers you a pet puppy and does not at least discuss neutering with you (most will insist on it, and a clause to that effect will likely be included in your sales contract), you might want to check into her references a bit more carefully.

Your puppy will come with a registration application that you'll need to complete before he is an officially registered purebred Min Pin.

Please don't consider telling a breeder that you want a "show puppy" with thoughts of breeding your pet. If a breeder has a Min Pin who she believes is "show quality," she will want to make sure that the dog is shown. If you are willing to take on the added responsibility of showing a dog (a very expensive and time-consuming activity), then by all means, discuss a show prospect. But if not, be honest and tell the breeder that you simply want a good-quality pet Min Pin to share your life and home.

Show-Quality Puppies

If you decide that you definitely want a show dog, you should choose a breeder who is successful in the show ring and who has a good reputation among her peers. Raising a show Min Pin is much the same as raising a pet, as you want them both to be well socialized and willing to walk on a leash with you, allow strangers to pet them, and to get along well with strange dogs. Your breeder may ask that you co-own this show-quality Min Pin with her until he has finished his championship. This will allow her to show the dog in the Bred-By-Exhibitor class at shows if you don't want to show him yourself, as well as have her name on the championship certificate sent by the AKC when your Min Pin has successfully completed his show career. Most breed clubs offer annual awards based on the number of championships acquired during the year, which is why many breeders do keep their name on as many of their dogs as possible. In return for this co-ownership, you should never be forced to breed a litter of puppies that you don't want, and the purchase price should reflect the fact that you are in fact purchasing only "half a dog." In the case of a co-ownership, you should get every aspect of the ownership agreement in writing to avoid misunderstandings later on. Make sure of what you're getting into, and be certain you are dealing with someone you can trust. It is always far better to outright purchase your Min Pin, but in the case of a beginner, sometimes that isn't possible. Remember, too, that there are no guarantees that a baby Min Pin is going to grow up to be a showstopper no matter how perfect he may seem now. Every person who shows dogs knows that sometimes the

Good Breeding

A responsible, professional, truly concerned and dedicated breeder will:

- happily answer all of your questions and will have questions of her own to ask you;

- offer a contract stating what both parties can expect from the transaction;

- be willing to take the Min Pin back if he does not work out in your home (most will even insist that this clause be part of their contract);

- give you not only the registration application for the puppy (or registration certificate for an older dog) but will also include a three- or four-generation pedigree and concise written instructions on how to take care of your new Min Pin;

- make certain the vaccinations and health checks are up to date before sending the Min Pin to his new home and have the entire litter temperament tested so as to be able to place each puppy in a home where he will be most appreciated;

- be able to state the qualities that the puppy possesses that make him a prospective "show-quality" puppy, an "obedience dog" or a "pet-quality" puppy;

- belong to, or be in good standing with, the national Miniature Pinscher club;

- be active in area dog clubs and events, including performance events (obedience, agility, hunting, and the like);

- be willing to discuss the problems of the breed openly, including genetic health problems, and tell you about any potential problems in the Min Pin you are considering;

- have performed all necessary genetic testing on her breeding stock and be willing to share the results with you;

- become your mentor.

Be wary of any breeder (or other person trying to sell you a dog) who doesn't do these things.

A responsible breeder has the best interests of her dogs and puppies in mind throughout their lifetimes and will want to be assured you'll take the best care of a pup as possible.

very best puppies develop far differently from what was expected. Make certain that your contract covers what will happen to the dog in case he doesn't end up as the adult you and the breeder anticipated.

You should be wary of a breeder who offers "show-quality" Min Pin puppies if she herself does not show dogs or if neither puppy's parents is a finished champion. Unfortunately, the phrase "show quality" is becoming a catchphrase for folks just trying to sell puppies. You should ask such breeders who evaluated these puppies and what their qualifications were for doing so. Most veterinarians, unless they themselves breed and show Min Pins, are not qualified to assess the breed standard quality of a puppy or adult Min Pin. A veterinarian can tell you whether the dog is healthy and can possibly determine if he is likely purebred, but she cannot evaluate a dog's prospects in the ring. Only someone who is knowledgeable about Min Pins, one who consistently and successfully breeds *and* shows this dog at AKC conformation events, or someone who is licensed to judge Min Pins, is qualified to determine a "show-quality" Miniature Pinscher.

THE DOG OF YOUR DREAMS

All Min Pins are cute and loveable, but not just any of these loveable dogs will fit into that initial picture you drew in your mind. Be patient. Explore all the possibilities, and don't let your heart make a decision that your mind isn't clear about. And the most important rule to remember? It's that choosing a breeder is as important as choosing the right puppy.

It's not hard to find a Miniature Pinscher puppy. The newspapers of almost every city will have multiple ads in their classifieds, as well as possibly having promotional ads from pet stores offering Min Pin puppies for sale. Again, it's time to do your homework. Don't buy a puppy from the first person who offers you one.

Finding a Good Source

The best place to find a serious breeder of good-quality Miniature Pinschers will likely be a local dog show. There are all-breed dog clubs in almost every large city across the country, and to maintain their status as an AKC affiliate, they must host dog shows in their area each year.

A dog show is a great event for the family; if you've never attended one, be prepared for an eye-opening day of fun. The local kennel club secretary should be able to tell you what time Min Pins will be showing on each of the show days (most dog shows are held in "clusters" of two, three, or four days of shows), so you can plan to be ringside to watch them strut their stuff. There are more Min Pins in some areas than in others, but almost every show will have at least a few in attendance.

After Min Pins have shown, you can strike up a conversation with the people showing the dogs who caught your eye and inquire about any current puppies or upcoming litters. The dog community is very tight knit, so most breeders are knowledgeable about what their peers have in the way of puppies or upcoming litters, and most are more than willing to steer a good prospect of a responsible home to someone else if they have nothing available themselves. Be sure to wait until after their Min Pins have shown, however, as nerves are tight before ring-time, much as an athlete would be tense before a big game. After the judging is over, most people will be more relaxed and willing to take their time helping to point you in the right direction. Of course, temperaments in breeders can vary as greatly as those in the dogs they breed, and it's possible that you'll run into someone who isn't very pleasant. If you happen to come across a breeder or exhibitor who is surly or rude, don't take it personally—just move on to the

What Is Inbreeding?

It is possible that you may have heard the term "inbred" when someone described dogs with questionable temperaments and multiple health problems. Inbreeding of dogs, when done with a good background of genetic knowledge, can create a far superior example of the breed. In fact, the safest pedigree is one that has several familiar names or kennel names in a four-generation span.

It's a fact of life that like begets like. Breeding two totally unrelated animals of the same breed gives you a gene pool that is as scrambled as that of any mixed breed. You can't be sure what you'll end up with in appearance, type, temperament, or health. However, if someone who is familiar with canine genetics has produced a litter of Min Pins with a pedigree that has an easily traceable lineage, you can be sure when you look at the pictures of those ancestors that your puppy has every chance of having their same stellar qualities—including the good temperament and healthy body that fits the standard set forth by the national Miniature Pinscher Club of America.

next person.

If you can't find a show near you or don't want to attend a show, responsible, dedicated, and reputable breeders can also be found through the local kennel club breeder referral, from area veterinarians, and simply by word of mouth from friends. The Internet is filled with websites with list after list of Min Pin breeders from every corner of the world (although on the Internet as well as in "real life," less honorable breeders must be weeded out from the truly dedicated professionals).

A "hobby breeder" of Min Pins will be your best bet to find a good puppy who is sound in mind and body. A reputable hobby breeder will be knowledgeable about the breed and will devote much time and energy to the breed she loves. She'll be someone who will provide good support in the years ahead. It's likely she'll have a waiting list for puppies, so you should be willing to wait. It may take as long as a year of waiting, but it will be time well spent.

The person whom you're looking for truly has the best interest of the Min Pin breed at heart. She doesn't mass-produce puppies just so she can always have puppies to sell to make money. She produces only litters that will further her own breeding program and that she will be proud to exhibit at dog shows and Miniature Pinscher specialty shows in front of her peers. She will work hard to produce a litter that is as healthy as possible, and because she herself will be keeping a puppy from that litter, she has a personal, as well as a professional, stake in the quality of the litter. The purchase price of one of her Min Pins won't be less than you might find elsewhere, and indeed in some cases may be more, but you will definitely be getting your money's worth. She will have lived with your puppy and watched him interact with his littermates; she will

A Background in Genetics

A good knowledge of canine genetics is essential to anyone who breeds a litter of puppies of any breed, and breeders of Min Pins are no exception. Although Min Pins, in comparison with a lot of other breeds, are generally healthy dogs, there are several genetic health problems that are seen in the breed. The more common genetic disorders reported in Min Pins include: patellar luxation (slipped stifles), progressive retinal atrophy (PRA), and Legg-Calves-Perthes disease. (Please see Chapter 8 for details on these conditions.) A good breeder will perform all possible genetic health testing and will have knowledge of genetic inheritance factors and the Min Pins in her pedigree. She'll be able to use all that information to avoid those problems to the best of her ability, and her puppies should live a long, happy, healthy life. (Nature can always toss a wild card into the game, but your odds are certainly better if the person dealing the cards knows all the rules.)

know that this exact Min Pin puppy is one who fits the description you gave her of what you expect from your new addition.

At the Facility

When you visit the source to look at available Min Pins (or possibly to meet her and her dogs to see if you are comfortable with each other before you discuss actually purchasing a puppy), you should be able to see and interact with the parent. (Because it is rare that the best genetic match can be found in the same house or kennel, often the father of a litter will be miles or states away, perhaps even across the ocean—so don't be alarmed if the sire is not on the premises.) You should, of course, be able to see the puppies, scratch their ears, and pick up their feet without any fear of being nipped. If any of them should snap at you, quickly thank the breeder for her time and leave. There is no excuse for selling any Min Pin puppy or adult with an unstable temperament, or for using a dog with a bad temperament in a breeding program.

When you go visit a breeder, take a careful look around. Her dogs should be clean, comfortably housed, and socialized.

Questions From One Who Cares

You'll know instantly when you come across a dedicated source for your puppy. She'll have just as many questions for you as you have for her. These questions will likely include:

- Have you owned a dog in the past?
- Have you owned a Min Pin before?
- Why did you choose a Min Pin now?
- Do you know about the disadvantages of Min Pins, as well as their good points?
- Do you have a fenced yard?
- Can you provide references from your veterinarian?
- Will you be willing to neuter your pet?

Don't be upset by her queries. Be thankful that she genuinely cares about the puppies she produces and wants only the best for them.

If you can't answer these questions honestly, you should rethink your situation. And don't think you can get around answering these questions with half truths or false statements. The dog world is a tightly knit network filled with breeders from around the country—and now, with the Internet providing a way to keep in touch with the punch of a button around the world, dog breeders stay in close contact with each other. If you tell a breeder that you have a fenced yard, you'd better have one! Even if you live across the country from this breeder, her friend who breeds Boxers or Collies or Basset Hounds may live just across town from you and be more than willing to drive by to check out your place!

Just as you should answer the breeder's questions, she should be equally open about answering yours, and she should be impressed that you cared enough to do your homework and know what questions to ask. You questions should include:

- Were the parents genetically tested for all the common genetic health issues known to Min Pins?
- Was the litter temperament tested?
- Why is this puppy (or adult) being offered to me now?
- What makes you think he is the right dog for my family?
- Where did this puppy spend the first six weeks of his life?
- Were either of the dog's parents shown in conformation?
- Has this puppy or adult had all vaccinations necessary for his age?
- What type of registration materials will I be given with this Min Pin?

You'll also want to ask other questions about the daily and annual care of the dog.

Buyer Beware

Whatever source you choose to purchase your Min Pin, there are things you need to look out for. Beware of any seller who does not seem interested in your background or who can't answer genetic questions about the breeding program. Puppies from that type of source will be far more likely to have genetic health problems than will puppies bred by a caring professional who has more than a basic understanding of genetics and is aware of and familiar with the genetic problems that may lurk in her bloodlines. A source may

"Tech Support"

When you buy an electronic device such as a computer, you are usually offered a warranty program that includes "technical support." A good source will offer that "tech support" with each Min Pin sold. The source will want to hear how this puppy who was so lovingly created is faring in his new home, good or bad. She will also be there to rejoice with you in the good times and willingly help you work through any problems that might arise.

brag about her "champion pedigrees" and use the term as a catch phrase in her advertisements, but she likely won't be able to tell you why particular dogs were bred to the others over the years, and she'll probably have to look several generations back before she finds that single champion she's bragging about. You should always be sure to inquire about genetic testing done on the parents, and ask what genetic faults and flaws have been seen in the dogs in this puppy's pedigree. (If she says there are none, the person you're speaking with is either uneducated about Min Pins and the dogs she's breeding, or she's just plain lying. I know of no pedigree of any dog of any breed that has a flawless genetic makeup.) A knowledgeable breeder uses a pedigree that she knows very well as a sort of blueprint to produce puppies who will have the best chance of avoiding those pitfalls in the future.

Breeders who can't tell you much about their puppies' ancestry or who seem more interested in selling the dogs than in finding proper homes for them should be avoided.

Continued questioning should help you determine whether the source is someone from whom you'd want to buy a dog. You might ask, for example, what she hoped to achieve by the particular breeding that produced a puppy you are considering. If she tells you only what colors she thought she'd get, how many puppies would be in the litter, or something else trivial, it's time to leave. Ask a serious Min Pin person that question, and you will likely be quickly bored by the genetic discussion that will follow as she describes how she chose this particular breeding to avoid certain genetic faults or health issues, or how she hopes to improve a certain aspect of her bloodline. A good source will be planning to keep a puppy from the litter to incorporate into her breeding program, and she can likely tell you where that dog will go to be bred years in the future. She may even have a long-term plan that includes the great-grandchildren of the puppy you see before you now. You want to make sure you find a source who has the skills to help you with any problems that arise in the future.

But He Has Papers!

The presence of registration papers should not be considered a "Gold Seal of Approval." It simply means that both parents are presumed to be purebred because a pedigree for each of the ancestors of your puppy was provided to the registration organization, and each following generation has therefore been declared "purebred" and issued its own personal pedigree. The registration does not denote quality, health, temperament, or any standard appearance by any other registration organization.

To put a "pedigree" in layman's terms—even a mixed-breed dog at the shelter could have a written pedigree, if someone knew who his parents and grandparents were. A pedigree is simply a "family tree." It does not denote quality.

No Matter Where You Buy...

Your puppy's short- and long-term physical and mental health should be your primary consideration before buying.

No matter where you find your Min Pin, he should be happy and perky and have clear eyes and ears and a clear nose. He should have no sounds of congestion in his lungs, and he should be plump without having a bloated belly. His belly shouldn't be coated with dirt, and it should be free of any pustules or sores that sometimes occur in poor living conditions.

You should receive the name and address of the breeder, and you should be able to talk to her to see exactly how your puppy was raised before you pay for the dog. If a source seems unwilling to share any information about the puppy other than a general sales spiel until she is paid, you should

Registering Your Dog

If you received a registration application with your puppy or a registration certificate with an older dog, it will be easy to get him registered in your name with the American Kennel Club or other canine registry. The previous owner should have signed in the appropriate place that she was transferring ownership of the dog to you and dated it accordingly. She should have been present when you signed the papers stating that you accepted ownership of the dog on said date and that you wish to be recorded as his present owner, residing at the address you include in the proper section.

After you fill in and mail the application to the registration office (the address will be plainly printed on the registration papers) with the appropriate fee, you should receive your registration certificate within four to six weeks showing you as the recorded owner.

If you were not given or promised registration papers or an application for registration at the time of purchase, it will be a good deal more challenging to get your Min Pin registered. If you want to exhibit in AKC performance events and you are certain that your dog is a purebred, you can obtain an Indefinite Listing Privilege number that will allow you to participate.

Very Young Puppies

Puppies under 7 (most say up to 12) weeks of age should not be sold, as early separation from the dam and littermates can be permanently detrimental both psychologically and physically to a puppy. In fact, many states have laws in place that make it illegal to sell a puppy before he is eight weeks old. The law is even stricter if the puppy will be crossing state lines. If someone offers you a pup who is less than eight weeks of age, and the person who offered him to you did not breed him, you should find out where the dog came from. It is likely that he was shipped to where you are illegally.

leave immediately. It's likely she has something to hide, and that something might well be a secret that will create future problems in any puppy she sells.

There will always be a market for well-bred, healthy, lovingly cared for Min Pin pets. And there will always be loving, caring professionals who continue to breed more than enough pets for the responsible pet-buying population.

GENERAL HOME PREPARATION

The phone rings, and....*it's time!* When you realize that the moment has arrived to pick up your Min Pin, the excitement can be overwhelming. Much as first-time parents suddenly realize the enormity of their situation as they enter the delivery room at the hospital, the first-time Min Pin owner is now faced with the realization that she is about to take on a long-term, full-time commitment. Aren't you glad you did all that homework so that you're prepared now?

After you learn that there's a puppy for you, it's a great idea to have each member of the family wear an old t-shirt or socks for a day or so. Then, use these articles of clothing to stuff a small pillowcase that you can put into a well-sealed plastic bag to keep the scents intact. Send this pillow to the breeder for the puppy to sleep with for a few days before your impending visit. Hopefully, by the time you arrive, the puppy will already recognize you and your family by your scent and feel comfortable with you taking him away from his home. Put this same pillow in the crate with him at his new home. By doing so, you'll help to make him feel comfortable and safe, as some of the scents of his old home and the Min Pins he left behind will cling to it as well.

You'll be amazed at how very much your active Min Pin puppy's actions will resemble those of a rambunctious human toddler, so if your house is already toddler-proof, you're a step ahead of the game.

Puppy-Proofing the House

Get down on all fours (or lower—think about how tiny a Min Pin puppy really is), and look around the room. Suddenly, all sorts of menacing objects come to view, particularly electric and phone cords that can cause a nasty shock or even death if chewed. The chocolate candy that rolled under the couch at your last party could

Before letting your Min Pin out in the backyard, be absolutely sure that it is safe.

mean a stomach upset, at best, if found by a snooping puppy. Because of a Min Pin's diminutive size, even small amounts can cause severe health problems—even death. Obviously, small knick-knacks that could be swallowed and prove a choking hazard should be moved to a higher shelf, and anything that won't be improved with puppy teeth marks should be either removed or moved to a higher location. Once your puppy arrives, you'll quickly learn not to leave clothing, shoes, socks, belts, or other assorted pieces of clothing lying about, as your devious little Min Pin will be especially attracted to them because they smell like his beloved human companion.

It's a good idea to not allow your Min Pin the full run of your home until he is better trained. Baby gates and other barriers are worth their weight in gold to the puppy owner, because they effectively keep the puppy out of areas that are not puppy-proofed. It's also wise to contain the unhousetrained puppy in a room with linoleum, vinyl, or other easily cleaned floor-coverings. Many a carpet has not only been irreparably stained during potty training but also shredded beyond repair by an unruly baby Min Pin with time on his paws and an overactive mind.

Puppy-Proofing the Yard

Not only must your house be puppy-proofed, but your yard should be thoroughly examined as well. Besides looking for obvious holes in your fence or places where the fence does not reach the ground (remember how tiny a Min Pin puppy is—it doesn't take much of a space to allow him to wriggle through to freedom), if your dog will be near your parking area, be sure to check your cars for radiator leaks. Antifreeze is deadly to animals even in very minute doses, and because of the sweet smell, it is very attractive to them.

If you have a nut tree in your yard, make sure that all the nuts have been picked up, as they can be a choking hazard. Bottles and bags of yard and garden fertilizers, insecticides, and other poisons should be kept out of your Min Pin's reach, and he shouldn't be allowed into any area that has been recently treated with any of the above. Many flower bulbs and common landscaping plants are poisonous to animals if ingested as well. (Go to Chapter 8 for a listing of plants that you should keep away from your dog.)

THE FIRST DAY

It's best to pick up your new puppy early in the day, because this will give him time to get acquainted with his new family well before bedtime. The first night in new surroundings is the hardest, and it

You will always remember the first time you see your puppy's face looking out at you when you pick him up to bring him home.

will be quite a bit easier on him if he already feels comfortable in this new situation. If most of the family is gone during the week, plan to bring the puppy home early on Saturday morning so that you have all weekend to get to know each other before he has to be left alone on Monday morning. Ideally, you should choose a minor holiday weekend so that you can have an extra day to spend together before your normal schedule takes you back to work and school. Better yet, make plans to take a few additional days off from work—the first days are a critical time for housetraining and bonding with your new dog.

Pack a tote bag to take along when you pick up your puppy, with items guaranteed to make the transition to a new home easier. You'll need to pack towels (both cloth and paper), as your Min Pin is likely to get carsick or have an accident during this first ride. Also, bring treats, a nice fresh chew toy, a squeaky toy, and maybe a large stuffed animal to remind him of his mom and littermates. Someone will need to either hold or keep an eye on your little bundle of joy during the ride in case he gets sick or starts to get overly nervous.

Try to keep the ride home as calm as possible. If you have children, make sure they don't fight over whose time it is to hold the puppy. They must learn early on that he's not a stuffed toy with which they can play tug-of-war. Remind them that even small children appear large and frightening to a baby Min Pin, especially because children are more prone to making loud noises and sudden movements than are most adults.

SUPPLIES

Your Min Pin will likely come to you with a packet of information as well as toys and other items from his breeder, so it's always a good idea to check with her first to see what things you'll need to purchase. Once you think your home and property is safe (and trust me, you only *think* it's safe; it's amazing what a mischievous and adventurous Min Pin can find in a supposedly puppy-proofed environment), it's time for the fun part—shopping for goodies for your new family member-to-be!

The Crate: Your Dog's Private Den

A wire dog crate or plastic airline carrier or kennel is the most important item to put on your list. Although some people believe

Avoid the Holiday Rush

Although advertisements are filled with pictures and tales of Santa delivering Christmas puppies, you should never bring a new puppy or other pet into your home during a major holiday. The stress and trauma of a new home is hard enough on a tiny Min Pin without factoring in extra company, overly excited youngsters, and all the rest of the trimmings that come with birthdays and other major holidays. Instead, if you decide you want to give a Min Pin as a gift, wrap a leash and collar and a note saying that a Min Pin will be joining your family soon!

that using a crate for a dog is cruel, nothing could be further from the truth—as long as it's used responsibly. Because dogs in the wild are pack animals that live in a den, the dog's kennel or crate quickly becomes his den—a safe place where he knows he won't be disturbed while he's eating or sleeping. You should reinforce this fact to your children so they learn to respect the dog's private time-outs. The puppy should not be confined continuously (except at night) and will soon learn to quietly tolerate short bouts of confinement. Besides the obvious benefits of using a crate at home, having a pet who is unafraid of being crated or caged will make trips to the vet and groomer much less traumatic for everyone concerned. It will also make you more welcome at hotels and motels when you travel if the manager can be assured that your pet will be crated when unsupervised.

Individual food and water bowls should be available for your puppy before you bring him home so you won't have to rush out and get them when he needs them.

Identification

Because you love your Min Pin, you'll want to do everything you can to keep him safe. Of course, you will see to it that he wears an identification tag that states your name and cell phone number on his collar. Such a tag, however, is no guarantee that he won't end up lost. Collars are easily lost or removed, with tags attached. Many people advocate having your dog tattooed for identification purposes, and while this can be useful, it is worth noting that tattoos can be altered with ink or scarring.

My personal favorite identification method is microchipping. Although it sounds like something from a sci-fi movie, microchipping is definitely the wave of the present in tracking down the owners of lost pets. No more painful than a vaccination, a tiny capsule about the size of a grain of rice is injected under the

Min Pin Supplies

Have the following supplies ready for your Min Pin when you bring him home:

- collar
- crate
- food and water
- food and water bowls
- grooming supplies
- identification
- leash
- toys
- treats

flap of skin on the back of the dog's neck. Veterinarians and shelters are provided with scanners that read the digital number on the chip inside the capsule. This number can be cross-referenced with your name and address. A microchip is permanent (although sometimes they can "travel" beneath the skin and be difficult to locate), and it cannot be removed or altered.

Other Essentials

Your shopping list should also include puppy food (purchase the brand your puppy has been fed up to this point), treats (for early training incentive), and puppy piddle sheets (if you decide to paper train first before teaching your dog to go outside). You should have been stockpiling newspapers in the weeks past; they come in handy for not only preventing potty accidents but also for lining dog crates in case of accidents. You'll also need a guillotine-type nail trimmer, a flat or rolled collar (not a slip or choke collar), some lightweight or retractable leashes (some retractable ones come with a flashlight on the handle, which makes nighttime walks safer and more pleasant), dishwasher-safe, nonchewable bowls (one each for food and water), good-quality pet shampoo and conditioner, and a pooper-scooper. Of course, you mustn't forget the fun stuff, either. Your new Min Pin will need some sort of chew toy to take his mind off all the things you won't want him to chew. Nylabone makes some chews that are suitable for a Min Pin's size and chewing power.

INTRODUCTION TIME

It's important to remember the changes that are going on in your tiny Min Pin's great big world. Obviously he is going to feel very bewildered and stressed by all these changes. To help him cope, leave him alone at first, and let him wander through your home uninterrupted, getting used to all the smells, sounds, and feels of his new surroundings.

Be very careful not to surround your dog with too many people or overwhelm him with attention for the first few days. You should delay any introductions to anyone who doesn't actually live in the house with you until he has had a chance to acclimate himself and consider his new surroundings "home."

Never leave children alone with a new Min Pin, particularly not with a young puppy or a rescue dog who may have issues of which you are unaware. Unless your children are older and well trained on how to behave around dogs, they should never be left alone with your pets. The most common reason for a dog to be returned or turned into a shelter is because "something happened" while children and dogs were alone together. Remember, dogs are not babysitters, and kids don't always use good judgment when dealing with animals.

The Beauty of an Exercise Pen

Purchasing a folding wire (or plastic) exercise pen for your Min Pin is an excellent idea. The pen can provide an area indoors where your Min Pin has room to move about, use the bathroom, and sleep while you are gone, or create a safe area for him to take care of his potty business outdoors.

A Min Pin's Toy Chest

Make sure that you buy a variety of safe toys for your Min Pin. The list of items that *don't* make good toys is extensive. This list includes children's toys made of soft rubber, fur, wool, sponge, or plastic that could be chewed into small pieces. It also includes stuffed animals that have eyes and noses made of plastic that can be removed and swallowed and items with hard, sharp points or attachments that can break off and be dangerous if swallowed.

Balls of string, small balls, cellophane, plastic baggies, and other small items can get lodged in your puppy's throat, causing him to choke or suffocate.

Finally, don't offer your dog your old shoes or other personal clothing items. Giving these items to your puppy will confuse him by teaching him that sometimes it's okay to chew your shoes and rip holes in your shirts. You can't really expect him to make the distinction between when it's acceptable and when it's not.

Meeting Your Other Pets

Puppies must have safe, appropriate chew toys upon which to teethe and relieve stress.

Introducing your new Min Pin to any animals already living with you may take more than a little bit of public relations work on your part. If you are

introducing a new Min Pin to an older dog or cat, you must take great pains that the puppy doesn't get scared or hurt during the introduction. Be sure that your original pet knows that he isn't being replaced, and give him lots of extra one-on-one attention and treats.

Identification—Don't Leave Home Without It

Always make sure your dog is wearing some sort of easily read form of identification whenever he's away from home, even for short trips to the grocery store or to the veterinarian. Microchipping is great if a dog ends up in a shelter, but having a tag with your cell phone number on it ensures that whoever finds him can easily contact you.

I recommend putting your cell number on the tag for several reasons. If you're traveling or if you're out searching for your dog, you won't be home to take a call. In addition, if your dog wound up in the hands of the wrong person, it would be difficult for that person to track down your home address using only a cell number.

If you're introducing a new older Min Pin, you can expect some grumblings and protestations, but allow the animals to work things out on their own terms. Only interfere if it appears that there might be actual bloodshed. Dogs are pack animals, and it is up to them to decide who will serve as the "alpha dog" in the group. Keep treats handy for both so that they see the introduction of the other as a positive experience, but don't allow the treats to become an issue that might prompt a fight. Be certain that you stay relaxed and happy. Your original pet will be carefully reading your demeanor, so if you appear apprehensive and worried, he will likely think that you are nervous because of the "interloper," and he may try to "protect" you from perceived potential harm.

TRAVELING WITH YOUR MIN PIN

Your Min Pin will learn the word "go" faster than almost any other word. And that word will usually be met with frantic scurrying and zipping around excitedly waiting to be taken to the car for a trip.

However and wherever you travel, always make sure that your Min Pin is a good ambassador for not only his breed but for dogs in general!

Road Trips

As a rule, Min Pins enjoy being in the car with you, and you'll want to start bringing your dog out with you frequently, particularly at an early age, so that he becomes accustomed to riding along. Most Min Pins don't suffer from carsickness, but if yours does, you can either treat him with a veterinarian-approved motion sickness medication or slowly acclimate him to the

Supervise any introductions between dogs.

With a collar, leash, and his own travel kit for longer trips, your Min Pin will be ready to join you wherever you may want to go.

car's movement by taking him on short trips and letting him outside frequently to walk on firm ground.

It's okay to open the window a bit to let your Min Pin get that "wind in his hair" sensation, but never open a window all the way, and never allow your dog to ride with his head out of the window. Not only is he likely to get a bug or other flying projectile into his eye, but having his eyeballs dried by the wind for any length of time can cause some long-term problems.

Also, letting your Min Pin run loose in the car is never a good idea. Not only is it dangerous for you both, but you run the risk of losing your dog when you make stops. A tiny Min Pin can easily escape when a car door opens, and he'll be tempted to leap out if he sees something or someone he wants to greet outside. In the case of an accident (which an unruly dog riding loose in car can easily cause), if your Min Pin is riding loose, he will be much more likely to suffer serious injuries. The safest place for your dog during car travel is either in a carrier or a restraining harness that works with the car's seat belt to keep him securely in his place. Remember that the passenger seat is not a good place for your dog to ride, even if crated, because he could easily be killed by the air bag deploying in the case of an accident. Air bags were designed for the average-sized adult; a Min Pin's head is obviously much lower than a human's and may be much closer to the dashboard as well. Since an air bag deploys very quickly, you can imagine how much damage one can do to a small Min Pin who won't stand a chance against the pressure.

Never leave your dog unattended in the car, even in cool weather. Even winter sun can warm up a car's interior to uncomfortable levels in a surprisingly short amount of time. Min Pins have such small bodies, with such a high metabolism, that they do not acclimate easily to extreme cold or extreme heat. Be sure to bring along a blanket for him to snuggle into during cold weather and an ice pack or frozen water bottle wrapped in a towel during summer weather.

Online Help

If you have problems finding a hotel or motel that accepts dogs, check out www.dogfriendly.com or www.petswelcome.com. You'll find many dog-friendly places to stay, and you can search by location.

Long Rides

If your road trip is a long one, remember to bring your dog's food and water from home. Changes in either can cause stomach upsets that can wreak havoc with travel plans. You should plan to stop often to let your dog stretch his legs and go potty. Don't forget to bring either a pooper-scooper or plastic bags to clean up after him, too.

Your Min Pin should have his own travel bag for long trips that includes a doggy first-aid kit (see Chapter 8), blanket, emergency rations of food and water, any regular medication (as well as a prescription from his veterinarian), and extra toys. Be sure to bring along a copy of his medical records and vaccinations in case of emergency, an extra leash and collar, a small bottle of spray cleaner to take care of any accidents, plastic bags for quick pickups, small travel bowls for food and water, and perhaps a lightweight sheet to put over the bedspread if your dog sleeps in bed with you at a hotel.

When staying overnight at a hotel, make certain that you leave the room in the same condition you found it. Don't allow your Min Pin to get away with doing things in a hotel room that he isn't allowed to do at home. And be sure you clean up after him outside as well—hotels and motels won't continue to accept canine guests if they leave a mess behind. If he will be left alone in the room (leave him crated to avoid trouble), put a "Do Not Disturb" sign on the door while you are gone. It's usually a good idea to leave the

television turned on as company for your dog; the noise will also mask any noise he might make that could disturb neighbors.

Air Travel

Because of his small stature, if you travel by air, you can take your Min Pin with you inside the cabin of most airlines. You'll need to carry your dog in a soft-sided airline crate made to fit under most airplane seats. If you think he will be uncomfortable during the flight or be afraid of the strange noises and sensations, you can ask your veterinarian for a mild sedative to give him before you take off. Most Min Pins, however, will happily spend their time in flight chewing on a favorite chew toy or nestled against their favorite snuggly toy. Just make sure that he gets accustomed to the crate well ahead of time to avoid any last-minute difficulties.

Be sure to call ahead to verify the airline's specifications for size and availability of room on your flight. Most airlines allow only a certain number of animals in the cabin on each flight. Let them know well ahead of time that you will be bringing a pet on board with you. When you check in at the airport, you will need a current health certificate that will include proof of rabies inoculation, as well as a signed health certificate from your vet stating that your Min Pin is healthy and sound enough to take to the skies.

If you are traveling outside the US mainland with your Min Pin, you should be familiar with any quarantine laws at your destination. Most countries have lifted their stringent quarantines, but many still require any incoming pets to spend a certain amount of time in a boarding kennel (usually of their choice).

WHEN YOUR MIN PIN CAN'T GO WITH YOU

Unfortunately, there will be many times that your Min Pin will not be allowed to travel with you. In those cases, it's imperative that you find a good pet sitter or a boarding kennel that you are certain you can trust. You should check out any boarding kennel with the American Boarding Kennel Association (www.abka.com) to see if it is approved. If the kennel that you are considering is not listed, make sure that you do a thorough check of the facility before you leave your Min Pin there.

If you can't find a family member or friend to pet-sit your Min Pin for you, you can hire a professional house- or pet sitter to take care of your Min Pin while you are gone. Obviously, before you leave someone with access to not only your Min Pin but also your entire home, you should check references and perhaps even do a background search (available online for a minimum fee) for a criminal record. To locate a pet sitter near you, you can call the National Association of Professional Pet Sitters at (800) 296-PETS.

No matter in whose hands you leave your Min Pin, leave contact numbers for yourself, your regular veterinarian, and an emergency veterinary hospital while you are gone. You should also leave complete, detailed instructions for caring for your Min Pin around the clock. Note that a qualified professional pet sitter should be both bonded and insured for the protection of everyone involved.

Your puppy will certainly miss you, but a trusted pet sitter can provide for him while you're away.

FEEDING

Your Miniature Pinscher

Before you brought your Min Pin home, you should have received notes from his breeder about what and when she had fed him and what she suggested for the future. That doesn't mean that you have to follow her guidelines forever, though. Times change, situations change, dogs change, and priorities change.

WHAT TO FEED MY MIN PIN?

Be prepared for myriad opinions when you ask the question "What should I feed my Min Pin?" One person may swear by the Bones and Raw Foods diet, another by home-cooked preparations, and still another will stand by her recommendation to feed the highest quality of prepackaged dog kibble supplemented with any necessary vitamins. One thing they'll all agree on, however, is that no matter what you feed your Miniature Pinscher, you shouldn't overdo it. A Min Pin's tiny frame simply cannot take a lot of extra weight. Obesity, although less common in Min Pins than in some other breeds, is a serious problem that you'll want to be sure to avoid.

Commercial Diets

Canned food, dry food ("kibble"), and semi-most food are all available commercially. While commercial diets sometimes get a bad rap from holistic pet owners, certainly no one can argue with their convenience and availability. And, many would argue, some prepackaged food is of unbeatable quality. Feeding one little Min Pin would seem to be a relatively simple matter to figure out—certainly dogs existed for centuries without the help of humans to keep their diet regulated—but the science of canine nutrition is a field of intense

The Min Pin Metabolism

Pound (kg) for pound (kg), your Min Pin will need to eat more than a Great Dane! Can you believe it? Researchers have proven that small dog breeds have a dramatically different metabolism than that of large breeds. Their studies show that a Great Dane weighing 100 pounds (45.4 kg) needs to consume approximately 25 calories per pound (0.5 kg) of body weight every day to maintain condition, whereas an 8-pound (3.6 kg) Miniature Pinscher must take in over 50 calories per pound (0.5 kg) of weight every day to maintain a healthy weight.

study and research. This research has led to commercially available diets of extremely high quality, and each year brings about new and improved recipes believed by most experts to be able to significantly add to the health and longevity of your dog. The choices are almost limitless.

Reading the Label

You can make an informed decision about the food your Min Pin will be ingesting if you learn to read the label on dog foods before you buy. Pet food labels are regulated by different rules than foods for human consumption, and you may have to do some homework before you totally understand what you're reading, but it's worth it to your Min Pin to make sure that he gets the best possible nutrition.

The product name is the first part of the label a consumer notices and can be a key factor in the decision to buy a product, especially if that person isn't well educated in reading and understanding the actual ingredients. Be a savvy shopper and pet owner and learn what marketing ploys are used to sell dog food, and don't fall for gimmicky names and advertisements.

Choose the highest quality dog food you can afford. There should be a list of ingredients on each package, as well as the

Be sure that your pup has a supply of fresh, clean water both indoors and outdoors.

percentage of fat and protein in a bag of kibble. The order of those ingredients is of great importance to the consumer—and it's vital to your Min Pin, whose life literally depends on what food you decide to feed to him.

The first ingredient that you should see on a premium dog kibble will be some sort of specific meat meal, and the kind of meal should be spelled out with precision. Look for chicken meal, lamb meal, pork, or beef, rather than just "meat meal," and you want to be sure it says "meal" after the type of meat, too. Whole meat is mostly water, so if you don't get meat meal, your Min Pin will be getting a poorer quality of food. For what it's worth, when choosing your pet food, consider that most canine nutritionists prefer a chicken-based diet, as dogs tend to digest chicken better than they digest lamb or beef.

Although no dog food company is going to advertise the fact, a lot of the foods listed as "by-products" are usually heads, necks, stomach contents, organs, and the like. Although that sounds unappetizing to us humans, this is the first part of a fresh kill that a dog will eat in the wild. Organs are higher in natural vitamins and minerals than other parts of the carcass.

Most Min Pin owners find that a high-quality commercially prepared kibble is the most convenient food choice for their dogs.

Because corn is usually one of the cheapest products to include in pet foods, you may see some type of corn product in the food. Some dogs can tolerate and process corn easily, while others can't. If your dog starts itching, licking his feet, getting ear infections, or showing other types of allergic reactions, and the food you feed has corn in it, this may be a signal that your dog isn't tolerating the corn. Wheat also tends to be an allergen with many dogs, as does soy.

You should also look for a label that has no chemical preservatives, such as ethoxyquin, BHA, BHT, or propyl gallate listed on it. Instead, look for food that is preserved with mixed tocopherols (which is vitamin E). You should be aware that dog food companies are not legally required to list any preservative that they themselves did not add. This does not mean, however, that the ingredients they have used in preparing the kibble were not preserved with chemical preservatives before combined into the final product. For example, Coast Guard regulations state that any fish meal must be preserved with ethoxyquin. Therefore, if you feed a food with a high fish meal content, it will likely have ethoxyquin in the final kibble even though it likely won't be listed on the label. The jury is still out on how bad ethoxyquin really is for your dog, but there is a lot of well-researched literature available on the subject. Do your homework so that you can make your own educated and informed decision.

You'll want to look for a statement on the dog food label stating that the Association of American Feed Control Officials (AAFCO) has confirmed that the dog food you are considering is complete and balanced for dogs of all life stages. This means that the food was actually fed to real dogs to determine that it meets the nutritional needs of your dog. Some food companies just determine the nutritional values in their lab, without ever feeding it to actual dogs. Their label reads more like this: "[Name of Dog Food] has been shown to be complete and balanced using testing procedures as outlined by the AAFCO." You can call the food manufacturer if the information isn't on the package, and ask whether its food was actually fed to dogs during an AAFCO-approved feeding trial or whether the numbers just add up correctly in the laboratory.

Remember that your Min Pin must have the right balance of nutrients—proteins, fats, carbohydrates, vitamins, and minerals. These nutrients must be in a form that your dog can digest. A Min Pin's metabolism is high, but there are still some things they cannot digest. Keep in mind when reading labels that although a meat meal may be the first ingredient on the list, suggesting it is the primary ingredient, the cereals and vegetables could still be added together and become the true primary ingredient. You should also be certain that the food you choose does not change its recipe according to which grains are cheaper during a particular season. In addition, never choose a dog food that is unnaturally colored just to make it more palatable to

Water, Water Everywhere!

How much your Min Pin drinks is as important as what he eats. Free access to fresh water at all times is essential for dogs. Your Min Pin can become ill and die quickly from dehydration if access to water is denied. High temperatures, exercise, and conditions such as lactation, diarrhea, and certain diseases can dramatically increase your Min Pin's water requirement. A rough estimate of the maintenance requirement for your Min Pin is approximately 1 ounce (29.6 ml) of water per pound (0.5 kg) of body weight per day. An otherwise healthy-looking Min Pin who is drinking three or more times this amount of water may have a disease, such as diabetes or kidney failure, and should be examined by a veterinarian. A dog who is drinking less should be tempted to drink more by putting something tantalizing into his water (such as beef broth or apple cider vinegar).

the human who is serving it. Your Min Pin won't care what color his food is—he only cares about its taste, smell, and texture. Some colorings are not only harmful to dogs, but they can cause hair discoloration.

What Commercial Food Is Best for My Dog?

Kibble is the most popular form of commercial dog food. Puppy kibble is richer in protein, fat, vitamins, and minerals (especially calcium and phosphorous) and is calculated to meet the rapid growth and metabolic rate of an active, maturing puppy. Puppy kibble is also suggested for pregnant or lactating females. Although most puppy food manufacturers and many breeders and veterinarians recommend keeping a young dog on puppy food for 12 to 18 months, there is a large contingent of veterinary researchers who now recommend progressing to adult food as early as six months of age. These researchers believe that most prepackaged puppy food is too nutrient dense and rich for dogs who are more than six months old, and they contend that this may actually contribute to orthopedic problems such as hip dysplasia and osteochondritis dessicans, as well as obesity, if continued for too long a time.

There is a popular consensus that high-quality adult/maintenance diets are desirable for most dogs from the ages of six months to six to eight years. After that point, senior diets possess fewer calories, more fiber, and an electrolyte and nutritional balance more suitable for older Min Pins. You should consider switching to a food formulated for seniors when your Min Pin reaches around eight or

It's important to feed a dog food that is appropriate for your Min Pin's age and activity level.

nine years of age, especially if he is less active or overweight.

If your Min Pin is overweight, there's a kibble designed just for him. Light diets contain fewer calories, less fat, and more fiber than standard preparations and may also contain fat absorbers or metabolic accelerators.

Performance foods, at the other end of the spectrum from light diets, are very high in protein and fat and are only appropriate for Min Pins on a rigorous, regular training schedule that depletes the system faster than most regular foods can replenish.

There are also prescription diet foods available from veterinarians for Min Pins with various medical disorders, including endocrine, gastrointestinal, urinary, and cardiac conditions that can be worsened by a diet of regular prepackaged foods.

Canned food has a higher water content than kibble and is more expensive. Canned food also doesn't give the teeth and gums the workout kibble does, and because small dogs are prone to dental problems, you might want to stick with dry food. Or you can do what some owners do and add a scoop of canned food to a bowl of kibble to make it more palatable.

Semi-most food tends to be full of sugar and preservatives. Although your dog may love the taste, it's really not the best choice for him.

Bones and Raw Foods Diet

Proponents of the bones and raw food (BARF) diet swear by its benefits, which include its ease of preparation. With the small portion size necessary for a Min Pin, you won't have to set aside much space in the fridge for his special diet.

Start with basics—raw, meaty bones. It is imperative that your Min Pin never receive any bone that has been cooked. A raw bone won't splinter, but a cooked bone almost surely will, which can cause not only gastronomical upset but can cause a blockage that will have to be corrected with surgery—and sometimes even emergency surgery isn't enough. It's not worth risking your Min Pin's life to allow him to have cooked bones.

The BARF diet should also include fish or eggs and fresh fruits and vegetables. Remember that your little Min Pin descended from wild pack animals that hunted for their food. Those dogs ate only the game they could catch and vegetable matter they found palatable. They rarely got sick, they lived long, healthy lives, and seldom did any suffer the maladies that today's overpampered pooches experience regularly. Dr Ian Billinghurst, a world-renowned veterinary surgeon and one of the greatest proponents of the raw foods diet, states firmly that 60 to 80 percent of a dog's diet should consist of raw, meaty bones.

For the majority of those who choose to feed raw foods, chicken is the basis of most of their dog's meals. It's easy to come by, it's inexpensive, and it's good for your Min Pin. If chicken isn't readily available to you, use what you can get locally, like lamb, beef, venison, duck, rabbit, pig, or raw whole fish—as long as it is raw

Doggy Stew

The following recipe is suggested by a long-time Min Pin owner who cooks two days a week for her dog and then freezes the food into daily serving amounts.

Doggy Stew

4 cups chicken or fish or lean ground meat (about 2 pounds [0.9 kg])

1 cup zucchini or other fresh vegetable, finely chopped

1 cup string beans, cut up

1/2 cup white potato

1/2 cup yam or sweet potato

Combine all ingredients in a slow cooker along with 4 cups (946.4 ml) of water. Place on the lowest setting and let cook all day while you're at work or while you're sleeping. Place in the refrigerator to cool. Skim off any fat that accumulates on top. Mix together well and keep refrigerated or freeze in daily serving sizes.

You can mix and match the vegetables according to what's on sale at the grocery store or farmer's market or what's available in your own garden. Min Pins seem to have a particular fondness for carrots, summer squash, green beans, and tomatoes.

Even if you decide that cooking for your Min Pin's every meal is too much for your schedule, you can still incorporate some good home cooking into his diet with these tasty doggy treats. Just be sure to label them "for the dog," although humans might find them pretty tasty, too!

and meaty and came from a good processing source, it will be good for your Min Pin.

Remember that your Min Pin does not have the right digestive system to cope with a lot of grains, so don't include them in your raw diet. Besides not digesting them well, grains are the biggest source of allergies in dogs. Grains make up the majority of a lot of prepackaged dog foods, and that's another reason to consider feeding a raw diet. You might also consider whether the beef you feed your Min Pin was feed-lot raised or grass-fed. For both humans and animals, beef from a grass-fed cow provides healthier meat. Most processors don't mark their beef as grain- or grass-fed, but some will be able to tell you if you ask them.

An added benefit to feeding the BARF diet is that your Min Pin will require fewer trips to the dentist to have his teeth cleaned. Most dogs who need regular dental cleanings are ones who are fed canned dog food or moistened dry kibble; feeding bones is a natural way to avoid plaque buildup on your Min Pin's teeth.

Dinner time is always a wonderful time in a dog-filled household.

Many people hesitate before feeding raw foods and eggs to their Min Pin, because they have heard the warnings about bacteria in raw food. While those warnings are applicable to humans, they don't apply to dogs. A healthy dog's stomach acid is exceptionally strong (think about the kinds of things a wild dog eats that don't upset his stomach) and is designed by nature to break down and destroy the bacteria that a human stomach could never tolerate. Also, the intestinal tract of a dog is short, and it is designed to move food quickly and efficiently, giving it less time to cause problems.

Before you start your Min Pin on an all-raw diet, you should discuss the diet with your veterinarian. If she discourages you and you're still interested, continue to do your own research, and ask questions of other vets, breeders, and owners. In my experience, some veterinarians don't receive much education on nutrition, other than that which is provided by commercial dog food companies. Obviously, none of those vets are going to suggest anything or believe in anything other than feeding prepackaged foods.

Pros and Cons of a Raw Food Diet

On the plus side, the overall condition of a dog, including his muscle mass, coat condition, and energy levels, usually improves when fed a proper BARF diet. A natural raw diet has been proven in many cases to eliminate some dog food-related problems, including problems with anal glands, heavy buildup of plaque on teeth, skin problems, allergic reactions, and weight problems.

In addition, you aren't feeding your Min Pin the artificial preservatives and colors contained in many prepackaged dog foods, and the diet is palatable to almost every Min Pin. Raw foods contain no rancid or questionable fats. An interesting relationship between raw foods and the way dogs eat has also been noted. Slow eaters seem to pick up their pace, and fast eaters slow down.

On the other hand, there are disadvantages to feeding a raw diet. For starters, if your Min Pin has been raised on a kibble diet, the switch must be done gradually to avoid problems with toxin release. A BARF diet is also less convenient than serving packaged dog food. A reliable source must be found, and the meat must be purchased and stored properly. It must be thawed before feeding, which takes more forethought and time than opening a can or scooping food from a bag. Vegetables should be juiced or ground before feeding, which can also be a time-consuming task.

Traveling can require more of a time commitment, because it is harder to carry or find a source on the road for meats. Most people who feed the BARF diet continue feeding 10 to 15 percent kibble so that their Min Pin remains used to it. Then, when they travel, they can feed a total dry kibble diet if necessary without bad side effects.

Home-Cooked Diet

In today's busy world, it's often hard to find time to cook for the family. Nonetheless, there is a surprising number of people who cook for their dogs. Many of these owners believe that the health benefits their dogs receive from home-cooked food make their

---

A Nutritious Treat for an Ill or Elderly Min Pin

Sometimes providing a sick or older Min Pin with enough fluids is a difficult task. This recipe should help you get adequate liquids into even the most finicky eater.

Pupsicles

Have 2 or 3 ice cube trays available

Ingredients:
2 cups (236.6 ml) low-salt beef or chicken broth

Sprinkle of garlic powder (not salt)

2/3 cup (157.7ml) water

Mix water with beef or chicken broth and pour into ice cube trays. Place in freezer and serve cold. For an extra treat, add a rawhide stick when the mixture is about half frozen.

efforts well worth it. Many dog owners choose to cook for their pets due to the increasing amount of literature that argues that "convenience foods" (prepackaged kibble) can be harmful to dogs for many reasons. This literature suggests that most manufactured dog foods contain too many grains and not enough meat product, that the dried kibble can expand in the stomach, causing problems with bloat, and that when research was done into the exact ingredients used, the results were shockingly inferior for all but the very highest quality kibbles. In addition to poor-quality food content, there are also unwanted contents in prepackaged foods, including BHA, BHT, and ethoxyquin. (All three preservatives have been proven harmful and may have a link to seizures, as well as other health issues.)

KEEPING IT INTERESTING?

One nice thing about feeding your Min Pin is that he really doesn't have to have variety in his diet for him to be happy and content. In fact, the opposite is true. Dogs don't look at cuisine the same way we humans do. They'll eat what's put in front of them and enjoy it, unless they are led to believe that by being finicky they can get something more tasty. Sure, they'd love to have a diet rich in tasty new snacks, but they won't sit around and pine if they're served the same thing every day.

If you're not sure if you're feeding your puppy what he most needs, consult your veterinarian.

Feeding your Min Pin table scraps is never a good idea, because they can upset a Min Pin's sensitive digestive tract and cause vomiting or diarrhea. This is especially true of spicy or fatty foods. In fact, fatty foods can induce a life-threatening disease called pancreatitis in susceptible dogs. Many adult dogs cannot digest milk products and will develop diarrhea if given them.

It's best to just keep your Min Pin's diet simple and plain and give treats that are designed for your dog's digestive system. If you insist on feeding your Min Pin table scraps or other rich "people food," this food should make up less than one-fourth of his total food intake each day. Scraps should also be a mixture of foods—plenty of vegetables, and not just meat scraps. And bear in mind that if you decide to start giving your dog treats from the dinner table, you inadvertently may be teaching him to beg.

HEALTHY DIET, HEALTHY DOG

You can tell whether your Min Pin is getting the proper nutrition from his food simply by looking at him. The exterior results of a dog's diet, plainly visible to the well-trained eye, are similar to the results of the diet on the dog's internal organs and working system. If you like what you see, you can be sure that your Min Pin is getting good nutrition, which is imperative for resisting infections and disease. If your Min Pin's eye color (the membrane visible under the lower eyelid) is light or white in color, it means that he may be receiving improper amounts of iron or other minerals in his diet, or he may not be assimilating these minerals well. If the color is normal (pink to red), he is receiving the correct balance, and his body is using the minerals properly.

Check your Min Pin's gums and mouth tissue (both color and texture). Gums that are loose on the teeth, are light in color, bleed, or have white spots indicate that your dog is not receiving proper amounts of (or is not assimilating properly) vitamins, minerals, and amino acids. Normally, the gums are firm on the teeth, there is no bleeding when they're rubbed, and they are a nice dark color.

The skin is also a good indicator of nutritional balance. Improper balances of protein and fatty acids can make skin dry and

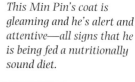

This Min Pin's coat is gleaming and he's alert and attentive—all signs that he is being fed a nutritionally sound diet.

Holy Mackerel Cakes

Not only is mackerel inexpensive, but it is also a fabulous source of protein and calcium. The bones are left in the mackerel when it is canned, but they are very soft and chewy and won't be a choking risk for your Min Pin.

Preheat oven to 350°F

15-ounce (425.2 g) can mackerel

cup whole grain bread crumbs

1 tablespoon minced garlic

1 tablespoon minced green pepper

2 teaspoons vegetable or peanut oil

1 egg, beaten

Using a fork, flake the mackerel and mash it thoroughly. Add the other ingredients and mix well. Shape into small balls and place on a greased cookie sheet. Using your fork, press each ball slightly to flatten it. Bake for about 20 minutes. Flip the cakes over and bake an additional five minutes to brown them on both sides and dry them out slightly. Cool completely and store in the refrigerator in an airtight container.

flaky and can cause your Min Pin to develop a condition known as "hot spots." The incorrect amount of these nutrients can also make a Min Pin's coat dry, brittle, and dull in color. Good skin is soft, smooth, and pliable, with no signs of dandruff, flaking, or moist eczema. When inspecting the skin, you should also check for the proper amounts of fluids.

Without proper hydration, the skin hangs on the body, seems stiff, and when pulled away from the body, retains the body's shape without smoothing itself back down to the contours of the body. Your dog's skin should "bounce back" if he is receiving the right nutrition.

Vitamins and minerals will also affect your Min Pin's energy and activity level, as well as his muscle tone.

HOW MUCH TO FEED

Regardless of what you decide to feed your dog, provide the amount that you and your veterinarian establish for your Min Pin. Note that if you choose to feed him a prepackaged kibble, the proper amount may not necessarily be what the label on the package suggests. Every animal has a different level of activity, an individual metabolism, and a different ambient environmental temperature. In addition, breed, age, and other environmental stresses all can impact daily requirements for an individual dog. Use the feeding guidelines on the bag of kibble as a rough starting point. Then do the math. If your animal becomes thin, feed him more often and/or in a greater quantity. If your pet is obese, feed him less.

When you're deciding how much to feed your Min Pin, be sure to factor in the number of treats he is given (or has stolen) during the day. Min Pins are consummate "vacuum cleaners," and they love to scarf up crumbs and snacks that fall to the floor. One owner came home to find her Min Pin snacking on cornflakes out of the box that had been left on top of her refrigerator. "How did he get *up* there?" she wondered. To find out, she eventually hid in her pantry, put a dog treat on top of the fridge, and watched while her precocious Min Pin jumped onto a table chair, walked across the kitchen table, jumped over to the counter, and then, using a set of large canisters as a sort of stairway, walked up to the windowsill, which he used as a springboard to jump up to the top of the fridge. Believe me, she made sure she left all chairs pushed well under the table from that point on!

Diet and Exercise

A Min Pin who receives less than one hour of activity a day will need approximately 300 to 400 calories per day (depending on his actual weight). Make sure you don't overfeed him, because his activity level isn't high enough to burn off the excess calorie intake.

A Min Pin who receives between one and two hours of exercise a day (considered the minimum for a Min Pin with their high energy levels) will need to consume between 350 to 500 calories a day. During cold weather, if he is outside much, he may require more calories to maintain a good weight, because the amount of energy

It's a Tasty Meatball

Feel like baking something special for your pet? These appetite pleasers are sure to bring a happy grin to the face of any Min Pin! You can double or triple (or quadruple, depending on your Min Pin's appetite) this recipe and freeze the leftovers (if there are any)

Preheat oven to 350°F

1/2 pound (0.2 kg) ground beef

1 carrot, finely grated

1/4 cup of any other seasonal vegetable, grated

1 tablespoon grated cheese (your dog's favorite flavor)

1/2 teaspoon garlic powder (powder, not salt!)

1/2 cup whole wheat bread crumbs (make a piece of overdone toast and crumble it)

1 egg, beaten

1 tablespoon tomato paste

Combine all ingredients and mix well. Roll into small meatballs and place on a lightly greased cookie sheet. Bake until the balls are brown and firm (about 15 minutes). Cool completely, and store in an airtight container. Keep refrigerated.

he needs to maintain a constant body temperature increases as the temperature drops.

If your Min Pin gets between two and three hours of activity per day, he'll need from 400 to 550 calories per day. Remember, if your Min Pin gets less exercise for a while due to illness or other circumstances, ration his food accordingly.

Obesity

Obesity isn't usually a common complaint within the Min Pin world, because most Min Pins are so energetic that they will usually manage to work off whatever extra food they consume. Most humans would love to have a Min Pin's metabolism, which keeps his waist trim and slim while he eats anything he wants. Unless there's some sort of underlying medical condition, an overweight Min Pin is usually the product of an overcompensating owner who doesn't allow her Min Pin to get the proper exercise or diet.

One way to assess whether your Min Pin is getting the nutrients he needs from his diet is to check the color and condition of his gums.

Feeding table scraps and low-quality food and providing constant access to food and too many rich treats are also significant contributing factors to a dog's weight problem. "Competitive eating" in multiple dog households (behavior that is not always apparent to the owner) may also be a factor in weight control. Add in the fact that few Min Pins get the daily exercise they really need, and it's no wonder that almost one-fourth of the dogs in the United States have problems with obesity.

In addition to overfeeding, obesity in the Min Pin may have physical, emotional, environmental, endocrine, and/or neurological components. Orthopedic conditions that are acquired, developmental, or present at birth may reduce the ambulatory capacity of the animal and predispose him to pain, which keeps him from getting enough exercise to stay trim. Hip dysplasia, osteoarthritis, a cruciate ligament, or a meniscal injury are not uncommon conditions that will deter a dog from getting enough exercise, and they can be a predisposing factor to obesity. Because some of these conditions can actually be caused by obesity, it is indeed a vicious circle.

Many Min Pins gain weight from problems related to metabolism. Metabolic disorders, including diabetes mellitus, hypothyroidism, hyperadrenocorticism (Cushing's disease), Addison's disease, and other endocrine abnormalities, influence energy and metabolism. Dogs suffering from one or more of these conditions often become overweight as a result of not having the energy to exercise, and even when they're strongly encouraged to do so, they may lack the necessary metabolic function to burn sufficient calories.

How much you feed your Min Pin depends on how often you feed him, how much exercise he is getting, and his overall condition.

If your Min Pin has a weight problem, your veterinarian may prescribe a high fiber/reduced calorie diet or advocate other dietary changes that focus on a decrease in overall caloric intake. She may also suggest a good exercise program. If you feel that your Min Pin is overweight, have him examined by a veterinarian, and discuss the options available for safe and effective weight management. Untreated obesity can be a devastating condition for your Min Pin, so instituting a diet and exercise program can add quality (and years) to your pet's life. (And because you'll be right there exercising with him, it can add quality and years to yours as well.)

Remember that a grossly overweight Min Pin isn't funny, cute, or anything other than pitiful. Obesity is the leading preventable condition that has a profound effect on a dog's health, well-being, and life span. It has been estimated that as many as half of all the pet dogs in the United States are overweight. Don't risk your Min Pin's life by allowing him to gain extra pounds (kg).

Nutrition and Longevity

In a March 2003 *Prevention* magazine article entitled "Add Years to Your Dog's Life…Help Your Dog Eat to Live, not Live to Eat!", researchers at the Purina Pet Institute in St. Louis, in collaboration with scientists from several major universities, published the results of a 14-year study. The research proved that a dog's life can potentially be extended by 15 percent when the dog is kept to his ideal body condition by carefully monitoring food intake. What better reason can there be to keep your pet on a strict diet? Not only will you add years to his life, but you will add life to his years as well.

Is Your Min Pin Overweight?

It's really difficult for most owners to accurately judge if their Min Pin has gained weight. Because we see him every day, we don't notice as the weight creeps up on him and he starts having a few more folds and wrinkles. Unlike humans, who have a love/hate affair with their bathroom scales, the only time your Min Pin will likely be weighed is when he visits the vet. If you have an otherwise healthy Min Pin who only sees the veterinarian for annual or semi-annual vaccinations and checkups, he may have developed a weight problem before you begin to see it creep up on him. Considering the health issues that go alongside obesity—whether as a cause or an effect—it's very important to keep a close eye on your Min Pin's waistline.

Wait! Dogs Have Waists?

They should! Stand above your Min Pin, and look down and check for his "waist." The basic rule is that the ribs should be felt but not seen. If you cannot feel the ribs, then it's very likely that your dog is overweight. (If you can see the ribs too clearly, your Min Pin may be underweight.) Overweight Min Pins also commonly have pouches of fat in the groin area between the hind legs.

From Pudgy to Perky

Few of us can afford a personal trainer to get our waistlines back to normal, but your pet should be able to count on you to get him back in shape. Here's how to do it:

- Cut out all treats and table snacks during the weight-loss period. Because the primary reason for obesity in dogs is overeating, divide the daily food allowance for your Min Pin into two to four small meals a day. Never free feed a Min Pin who has a weight issue.

• Weigh your Min Pin at the same time of day at least once a week. Keep a weight record.

• If you have multiple dogs, feed them one at a time, or feed them in separate crates or in separate rooms. A determined Min Pin on a diet will try to move to the bowl of his housemate to get more food. Feed your Min Pin before you eat, and then keep him in another room during meals to discourage begging.

• Restrict your Min Pin's unsupervised outdoor activity so that he may not scavenge for food when outside. Make sure that indoor and outdoor rubbish bins have secure covers and that any food left for wild or outdoor animals is kept out of reach of your dog.

• Tell your neighbors and visiting friends about your dog's weight-loss program to avoid having them feed your dog when he complains to them that he's starving.

• Always provide your dog with plenty of clean, fresh water. Exercise your Min Pin on a regular basis, starting slowly with short activity periods and gradually increasing the exercise time. Begin with walking, and when your pet shows signs of increased fitness, move to games that require running, such as fetch. You'll find that the added exercise with your Min Pin will help you maintain better health for yourself.

Min Pins tend to have a high metabolism, reducing their tendency to become obese.

FEEDING SCHEDULE

When determining your dog's feeding schedule, ask your veterinarian and the person who bred your Min Pin what type of regimen they suggest. In general, small-breed dogs require more food per pound (0.5 kg) of body weight than large-breed dogs because of their higher metabolism. Also, because a Min Pin's stomach is quite small, he can't assimilate large amounts of food at one seating. Some adult Min Pins may only need to eat once daily, but most do better if fed twice per day, morning and evening.

Some people who have only one Min Pin will "free feed." This means putting a bowl of food down and allowing the dog to snack throughout the day. While this lack of schedule works for some dogs, it isn't a good idea for either the Min Pin who bolts his food or the one who's a picky eater.

If you're starting out with a puppy, his feeding schedule needs will be far different from that of an adult. A puppy who is 6 to 12 weeks of age should be fed up to four times a day. Your veterinarian can suggest any supplements he may need to get his body off to a good start. After 12 weeks of age, you can begin feeding three meals a day until he is 6 months old. From six months to a year, he should be fed twice a day. If the twice-daily feeding works well with your schedule and your Min Pin is staying healthy, you might consider retaining that schedule for life. Frequent, small meals are better for your dog's digestion.

While it's a good idea to have a schedule for feeding times and to establish a general routine, be careful to continuously vary the mealtimes just a bit to avoid creating a "creature of habit syndrome." You'll find that your Min Pin will be quick to adjust to a regular feeding schedule and to a specific food composition. This can create big trouble if you ever have to deviate from their schedule. If you feed your Min Pin every

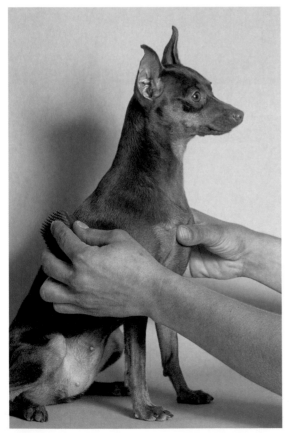

Giving your Min Pin a careful going-over on a regular basis will help you gauge whether he's too thin or too fat.

day at exactly 6:00 p.m. and always feed him exactly the same food, your dog's gastrointestinal system will soon program itself to start a digestion process at exactly that time.

Special Needs for Senior Dogs

As Min Pins get older, their diet needs vary. A Min Pin is considered a "senior" at nine to ten years of age. Senior Min Pins need less energy food than younger dogs, and they sometimes can have a poor appetite as they age. The best type of food to feed senior Min Pins is one that they find delicious and that is highly digestible; however, it should also have the right balance of nutrients to allow for his reduced energy requirements.

Because your pet cannot digest fats as easily during his senior years, great care must be taken to choose a diet that will contain the correct amount of calories to maintain his weight, without the addition of excess fats that can add to the problem of obesity. It's definitely worth the investment to purchase special dry foods formulated for the older pet. Small amounts of lean hamburger, cottage cheese, or yogurt are excellent additions to a senior pet's diet. Special foods may also specifically treat diseases and ailments that affect many seniors, including heart and kidney failure. It's important that these foods only be given on the advice of a veterinarian after a firm diagnosis has been made. Your vet may also suggest dietary supplements or vitamins to add years to your pet's life, and again, life to your pet's years.

The Min Pin's Meals in a Nutshell

While the exact quantity you feed your dog will have to be adjusted according to his specific needs, some good rules of thumb for feeding include:

- Growing puppies need: about 1/2 to 1 ounces (14.2 to 28.3 g) of dry, premium dog food per pound (0.5 kg) of body weight every day. This is distributed throughout three to four meals, depending on the age of the puppy.

- Adult dogs need: 1/4 to 1/2 ounces (7.1 to 14.2 g) of dry dog food per pound (0.5 kg) of body weight every day. Adult Min Pins can usually eat just one meal per day, although feeding twice daily is preferable.

- In addition to the dry dog food, a small amount of canned dog food can be added. If you are using quality dry and canned food, a good ratio is 2/3 dry to 1/3 canned.

- Nutritional supplements should not be necessary if your dog foods are of the premium variety.

5

GROOMING
Your Miniature Pinscher

At first glance, it might seem unnecessary to set aside an entire chapter devoted to grooming a Min Pin. Somehow "grooming your dog" brings to mind a picture of a Westminster dog show exhibitor carefully fluff drying and scissoring a Poodle. Aren't Min Pins "wash and wear" dogs? Who'd know if you didn't groom your Min Pin? Well, first of all, your Min Pin would know.

WASH AND WEAR DOGS? NOT QUITE...

Don't listen to the hype that Min Pins are "wash and wear" dogs. Indeed, they may not require the hours of brushing time that their longer-haired cousins require, but any good grooming session should be more than a cursory bath and a pat on the butt as the dog is put into a crate to dry. Spend time with your Min Pin. Make sure he knows that grooming time is quality time. Yes, it's mainly done for the aesthetic value of knowing your dog is clean and in good condition, but grooming time is also a time of bonding, as well as a time to check him for lumps, bumps, and cuts or bruises that might go unnoticed during regular petting or play.

One look at a dapper little Min Pin with his short, sleek hair, and it's obvious that he is never going to need much in the way of haircuts and trims to keep him looking well groomed and sharp.

The supplies you'll need to groom your dog include:

- bathtub or laundry tub
- conditioner (if necessary or desired)
- cotton balls
- ear cleaner
- hair dryer
- handheld spray attachment for shower
- nail clippers
- petroleum jelly or mineral oil
- rubber mat for tub
- rubber mitt
- shampoo (pH-balanced for dogs)
- shedding blade
- toothbrush
- toothpaste
- towels

However, you should never neglect your Min Pin's grooming or consider it unimportant just because he won't need the in-depth brushing, combing, trimming, and sculpting that some other breeds require.

The average Min Pin won't develop a strong "doggy" odor and likely won't need frequent baths unless he gets into something nasty. In fact, bathing a Min Pin too often is hard on his skin and coat, and you can do more damage than good. If your dog doesn't smell good, check his teeth and ears; don't just assume that any odors are coming from the skin. Sometimes, an unpleasant odor is a warning signal of a potential health problem rather than just the need for a bath.

SKIN AND COAT CARE

Far from being strictly a "wash and drip dry" kind of dog, a Min Pin's coat and skin needs regular attention. Although he doesn't have long flowing hair that requires daily brushing to eliminate mats and tangles, a Min Pin still needs regular brushing and attention paid to his skin, especially when he is shedding (which for some Min Pins may never seem to happen). Instead of the usual slicker or pin brushes seen in use on coated breeds, a small shedding blade, rubber mitt, or coarse wash cloth will work wonders on your Min Pin's coat, keeping him glossy, shiny, and healthy looking. By removing dead and dirty hair and stimulating the skin, grooming also helps your Min Pin to avoid getting skin infections and irritations. You'll find that if you keep your Min Pin well groomed, he'll be happier, because you'll be more likely to include him in family activities instead of leaving him behind because he needs a bath.

Shedding

All breeds of dog shed, but many factors go into how much is shed and when. Seasonal shedding, controlled by the amount of daylight, is normal for most breeds, with the most hair being shed in the spring and fall. Other influences include nutrition, surgical stress, and the general health condition of the dog. Overall, Min Pins seem to shed less than some other breeds, and with proper nutrition (feeding a good-quality food along with any supplements your veterinarian suggests) and grooming practices (which include using the correct tools as well as setting a frequent schedule for grooming), you can do a lot to diminish the amount of loose hair you'll find in your home and on your clothes.

Pest Control

Grooming is not just essential for healthy skin; it also makes you aware of any skin problems that may be developing. You should also use your grooming time to look for external parasites that your dog may have picked up on his latest foray into the great outdoors. Many Min Pins are prone to flea allergies, which can cause not only mild to severe discomfort but which can also create a staphylococcus infection that can be quite difficult to eliminate. Finding the problem quickly (you'll find that daily checks all over your dog's body are imperative during flea season), getting rid of the fleas efficiently, and promptly treating any resulting irritation or infection can help keep your dog's skin and coat in perfect condition. Not only can flea allergies and the resulting infections be hard on your dog's skin and coat, but they can also do quite a bit of damage to your wallet. The antibiotics necessary to combat infections of the skin are some of the most expensive of the commonly prescribed veterinary medications.

Because newly hatched fleas are

A rubber mitt provides stimulation for the skin while removing dead hair.

so tiny, you can't always depend on your naked eye to find fleas when you're grooming. Use a fine-toothed comb or a flea comb made specifically for this purpose. If you don't find any live fleas but are encountering tiny

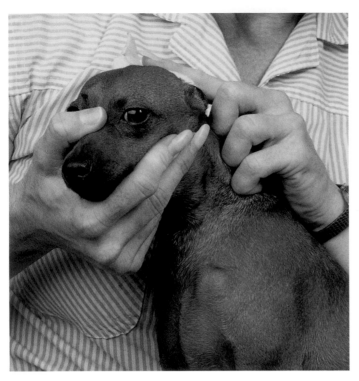

Pay particular attention to areas where pests like fleas and ticks may hide, such as around the ears and tail.

black grains of dirt, your dog does indeed have fleas. The black specks aren't dirt (or eggs, as some people believe) but rather are dried flea feces. Moisten them and you'll see the redness as the dried blood in the feces becomes hydrated. If you're shampooing your Min Pin and you notice that the water has a pink tinge, fleas are the culprit. You should either use a shampoo designed to kill fleas (in a pinch, you can use a dishwashing detergent that has lemon or another citrus juice), or follow a bath with a flea dip. Once the immediate problem has been taken care of, ask your vet what once-a-month flea preventive she suggests for dogs in your area. Remember, no dog who has fleas is going to have healthy skin, and unhealthy skin cannot grow a healthy coat.

Healthy Skin and Your Dog's Wellness

A dog cannot be considered "well groomed" unless he has healthy skin. If you notice any anomalies of the skin during your grooming session, alert your veterinarian immediately. A dull coat, combined with dry, itchy, or sore skin can be a symptom of something far worse than a need to increase the nutritional value of your dog's food and the number of grooming sessions. A malfunctioning thyroid, for instance, can quickly give your Min Pin's coat a very poor appearance. Brushing and rubbing your dog using the proper tools will not only help eliminate dead hair that would have eventually ended up on your carpet or wool blazer but will keep his skin soft and supple.

SPLISH SPLASH I WAS TAKING A BATH

How often to bathe your Min Pin will depend on your personal expectations and preferences, the type of skin and coat your Min Pin has, and the kinds of activities he engages in. It may depend on his general health and age as well, because some dogs' skin tends to get oily and retain dirt more easily as they get older, requiring more frequent baths. The rule of thumb should be to only bathe your Min Pin when he is truly dirty or has body odor. (Don't forget to check your dog's teeth and ears and not just assume that all odor comes from the body.) Too-frequent baths can do more harm than good, because they can dry the skin's natural oils. Skin that is overly dry can lead to scratching, and scratching can lead to bacterial infections and "hot spots." If you're a fastidious owner who insists on bathing your Min Pin more often than once a month, be sure to use a shampoo that has aloe or another skin treatment, and follow with a good skin-conditioning coat dressing.

Oily, Normal, or Dry?

Ask your veterinarian what shampoo she suggests for dogs who have the type of skin and coat that your particular Min Pin has. Some Min Pins will be prone to dry skin, some to moist, and some to oily. There is no specific shampoo or conditioner or combination of the two that will be right for every dog. Just be sure to use a shampoo that is pH-balanced for a dog's skin, which is very different from the skin of a human.

Most Min Pins don't shed very much, but in the spring, you may notice extra hairs on your furniture.

While using a shampoo designed for humans may be fine from time to time, it's best to use shampoo specifically made for dogs. The shampoo we use on our hair can create a pH imbalance in your Min Pin's skin.

Bathing Tips

Bathing a dog doesn't take a lot of skill or talent, but having the right tools and some basic information can certainly make the job a lot easier. To make bath time a happy time for both you and your Min Pin:

• *Have all your bathing equipment*

The Dreaded Shed

Min Pins don't shed as much as some breeds, but even though they're tiny, when it's time for them to shed, you'll swear they are losing enough hair to knit an afghan. All dogs shed to some extent year round, but the hair-shedding cycle is a lot more predictable for wild dogs and wolves, whose body cycles depend on the temperature and amount of light during each day to know when to drop their heavy winter coats and don their new springtime fashion. With the modern lighting and climate-controlled air in our homes, a dog's shedding cycle can get somewhat confused. The prime shedding season should always be springtime, when your Min Pin should in essence take off his winter coat and put on shorts and a t-shirt for summer. You'll notice that his summer coat may seem a little coarser than his softer winter coat. That's because most short-haired dogs grow stiffer hairs in the summertime, with extra space between each hair to allow air to better cool the skin.

Light and temperature aren't the only factors that determine when your Min Pin will shed. Hormone fluctuations, diet, illness, or stress can all do a number on your dog's skin, causing it to let go of hair at times other than the usual shedding season. If your Min Pin seems to be shedding more than normal, you should use a soft or rubber curry comb or brush on him to keep the hair in a brush where it belongs instead of wafting all over your home.

within arm's reach before you start. Don't force your shivering Min Pin to sit in a tub while you round up shampoo, towels, and conditioners. If you leave him there alone while you go traipsing off to collect your gear, you can expect to have a rodeo on your hands as you chase your Min Pin through the house to wrangle him back into the tub.

- *If you don't have a handheld sprayer in your bathtub, get one.* You'll be amazed how much simpler bathing your dog will be when you can actually spray water directly on him instead of having to pour it over him. Actually, because of their small size, many people find that they can give baths more easily in their kitchen sink.

- *Place a rubber mat in the bottom of your tub.* A Min Pin who is slipping and sliding around the tub is going to be an unhappy dog who will do his best to escape his slippery torture chamber. Being able to keep his feet firmly planted in place will make him feel more secure and will allow him to stand quietly as he's scrubbed.

- *Only use lukewarm water.* Just like Goldilocks' porridge, you will want the water to be not too hot and not too cold but just right. In the summertime, your Min Pin might enjoy being bathed out of doors using the garden hose, but don't attempt it in cooler weather. Not only will your Min Pin have a negative association with bath time, but you also run the possibility that he will catch a cold.

- *Place a cotton ball inside each of your Min Pin's ears, but not too far inside.* A cotton ball in each ear will help keep water from draining into the ear canal and thereby diminish the likelihood of an infection. The most common cause of ear infections for Min Pins is from water left in the ears after a bath. If you think you may have inadvertently allowed some water to seep around the cotton balls, you can put a couple of drops of alcohol in each ear and rub thoroughly to dry any moisture that remains.

- *Put a dab of petroleum jelly or a few drops of mineral oil* in your dog's eyes to keep any soap drips from burning them and possibly causing irritation.

- *Be sure you work the shampoo into a thick lather,* and scrub every bit of your Min Pin's body. If he doesn't like having his face scrubbed, try doing that with a washcloth and a tearless shampoo. If you're using a flea shampoo, wash the face first, and then work your way back to his tail.
- *Use a shampoo that is formulated for your Min Pin's skin and specific needs.* (Ask your vet or your breeder for her recommendation based on your particular Min Pin.)
- *Rinse well.* Shampoo left in the hair and on the skin can cause a severe skin irritation. Cover your dog's eyes with your hand while you're rinsing to avoid getting shampoo spray in them, tilting his head backward to keep any drips from running into his eyes or ears.

Shampoo

Choosing a shampoo is of the utmost importance. Using harsh shampoos can dry out your dog's hair and create static electricity, but using a shampoo with too many moisturizers can actually oversoften the coat, making it appear limp, lifeless, and oily. Experiment with shampoos (especially well before show day if your dog is being shown in conformation) to find one that provides the best cleansing agents along with the proper amount of moisturizers and conditioners. Even a tough little Min Pin coat needs a moisturizer or conditioner during winter months, especially when hair shafts can become dry and brittle.

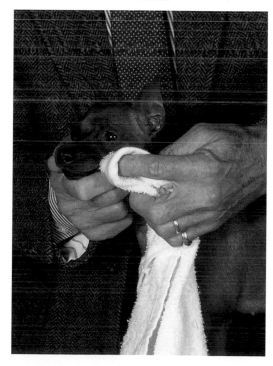

Go over your Min Pin's face with a damp cloth after a bath.

Drying

Never dry your dog with a hair dryer for humans unless the dryer has a "cool" or "air-only" setting. The average human hair dryer produces air that is heated to about 300°F (149°C). Be sure to keep the air vents unclogged in any hair dryer (for humans or animals) that you use, as a clogged air vent creates vastly hotter air than a dryer that has air moving freely through its vents. A hair dryer that overheats will cause more than just one "bad hair day." Dog hair (or human hair, too, for that matter) that has been exposed to too much heat will form gas bubbles in cavities in the hair shaft that are actually an early stage of combustion. Prolonged exposure to this heat will leave your pet with brittle and totally unmanageable hair.

When you are finished bathing, remove the cotton balls from your Min Pin's ears. Squeeze the excess water from his body, legs, and tail. Damp-dry his coat using old towels. In warm weather, your Min Pin can be allowed to air dry almost anywhere, but in cold weather, it's a good idea to place his crate near a heater or other warm air vent until he has dried. If you *must* use a hair dryer (on the coolest or "air-only" setting), be aware that most dogs must be trained to accept them.

Let the River Flow

You should always use lukewarm water when bathing your Min Pin, as hot water can shock the hair, and cold water does not do as good a job of penetrating the hair shaft. The most common mistake made when bathing a dog is not wetting the hair down thoroughly enough. Water is the dispersing agent for your shampoo—it distributes the shampoo and swells the hair shaft. This swelling helps open the cuticle to allow better penetration of the shampoo and conditioners. You should always wet the coat, wait for a couple of minutes for the water to absorb into the coat, and wet again.

THE EYES HAVE IT

Because they are fitted so tightly in the sockets (unlike those of a Basset Hound, for example), the Min Pin's eyes are usually not prone to irritation. That said, you should always check your dog's eyes as part of your grooming routine. Unless he has an infection, you will not need to clean his eyes regularly. When you give your dog his regular grooming and bath, you should put a small amount of mineral oil in or petroleum jelly around his eyes. This will protect the eyes from any debris, loose hair, or shampoo that might get into them. Although mineral oil can't be considered a cure for dry eye, it does lubricate the eye and can help avoid infections.

EAR CARE

Because of the set and carriage of a Min Pin's ears, they are less prone to ear problems than breeds with long, floppy ears that hang close to the head. This doesn't mean, however, that they can't suffer the same infections and other ear maladies that bother other dogs.

Keeping your Miniature Pinscher's ears clean as part of a regular grooming session can go a long way toward eliminating health problems that originate in the ear canal. In fact, while you're cleaning your Min Pin's ears is a good time to look for ear mites, fleas, and ticks. Ticks seem especially attracted to the folds of most dogs' ears, and smaller ones can hide quite handily, so be certain you look carefully inside all nooks and crannies.

Using a mild astringent or foaming ear cleanser (available from most pet supply stores or your veterinarian), you should clean out your Min Pin's ears each week. There are many good home "recipes" available for making homemade ear washes, but you should always check with your veterinarian before using them on your pet to be sure that they don't do more harm than good. Some dogs have more sensitive ears than others, so it's a good idea to use any product with caution, even after getting a green light from your vet. Watch closely for excessive redness or any discharge the first few times you use any ear-cleaning product. Apply whatever solution you choose liberally to the inside of the ear and massage gently, making sure the solution goes deep into your Min Pin's ear. Then use a tissue, cotton ball, or baby wipe to clean away the residue.

You should start cleaning a puppy's ears as soon as you bring him home so that he'll get used to the treatment and learn to enjoy it. Be warned, though, that as soon as you take your hand from his ear, your Min Pin will likely shake his head, which can

This Min Pin is becoming familiar with his owner's grooming tools.

splash you with dirty solution. Keep a towel handy to quickly cover his head if you feel a shake coming on.

Ear Cropping

Your Min Pin's breeder will have made the decision whether to dock your puppy's tail and remove his dewclaws when he was just a few days old. Very few Min Pins are seen with an undocked tail. However, it will be your decision as to whether you wish to have your puppy's ears cropped or leave them natural. The United States is one of the few countries in the world where cropping of ears and docking of tails has not been banned under "cruelty to animals" laws.

Ear cropping is a personal decision, and most pet owners opt to leave the ears natural rather than subject their "baby" to the pain and discomfort of major surgery simply for cosmetic reasons. There is no medical reason to crop a dog's ears; it is strictly done for aesthetic purposes. (Some proponents of ear cropping state that a Min Pin with cropped ears will have fewer ear infections than one whose ears are left drooping. You should ask your veterinarian her opinion about the health benefits of cropping.)

If you decide to have your Min Pin's ears cropped, ask your breeder or other local Min Pin owners for suggestions as to the choice of veterinarian to do the surgery. A crop that is incorrectly performed will leave your Min Pin literally scarred for life. Nothing can replace ears that are cropped too short, and it is far too risky to put a young animal back under anesthesia to repair mismatched or misshapen cropping. You should be sure that the veterinarian you choose is not only well trained and experienced in ear cropping but is especially experienced in cropping a Min Pin's ears. It should be stressed again that Min Pins are not miniature Dobermans, and their ear crop is unique to *their* specific breed.

Some Min Pins will still carry their ears erect even if they are left uncropped, but many will have ears that are "tipped" or folded forward about halfway up the length of the ear. Only those dogs with an improper ear set will have ears that flop close to their face (like those of a spaniel or Basset Hound). A Min Pin who has uncropped ears can still compete in AKC conformation competition, although it is likely that a dog with cropped ears could be considered more favorably by some judges than a dog who is shown in a natural state.

The cropping procedure is major surgery, done under general anesthesia. Portions of the ear are cut away, the edges are stitched back together, and the ears are taped into "racks" that must stay in place until the ears are trained to stand on their own. If a Min Pin is poorly bred, even the best cropping job may not stand up. If you have never owned a dog before that went through the cropping/taping process, you may likely find it more involved than you wish to consider, unless you plan to show your dog in conformation.

In addition to the risk that always exists when you place a dog under anesthesia, ear cropping surgery involves a good deal of lost blood. And as with any major surgery, there is pain involved. The post-operative care of the ears will be very time consuming for you and your Min Pin. He will have to learn to allow you to change the bandages and retape his ears around the racks until they are well trained into place. You will have to be committed to daily care of his

Anal Sac Cleaning

While your Min Pin is in the bathtub is a great time to express his anal glands. Probably the messiest and most unpleasant part of any dog's grooming routine is emptying these anal sacs, which are located on either side of the anus. They should be checked and emptied regularly to avoid impaction and infection. If you see your Min Pin scooting his rear end across the floor, it's likely he has either impacted anal sacs or an infestation of internal parasites. (Parasites often cause irritation of the anal sacs.)

The sacs are cleaned by holding the dog's tail up and gently squeezing each sac from the skin while pulling slightly outward. The smelly contents of full sacs will often squirt out under a great deal of pressure. The oily contents are not only foul smelling but will stain almost any cloth they come in contact with, so be sure you cover your dog's hindquarters with an old towel until you become somewhat adept at the procedure. If you need assistance learning how to express the anal glands, ask your veterinarian to show you how it is done. You should be sure you know what you're doing before you attempt it, because applying too much pressure can bruise the area and cause your dog a great deal of pain.

ears for as long as it takes for them to heal completely and be trained to stand correctly. Your failure to follow through with the proper care after cropping can lead to ears that refuse to stand, and your Min Pin will have been through the risk, the pain, and the emotional trauma for nothing. Accordingly, I would counsel you to think very hard about whether your Min Pin's ears should be cropped—particularly if he does not have strong potential in the show ring.

DENTAL CARE

Just as we brush, floss, and visit our dentist regularly, we should provide our dogs with similarly good dental care. It's very important that your training program include teaching your Min Pin the things he will need to know to make grooming time easier, such as allowing you to look inside his mouth and accept your touch on his teeth and gums. Each time you groom your Min Pin, you should look closely at his teeth, watching for a buildup of plaque or tartar or any loose or missing teeth, as well as bleeding gums.

Keeping Teeth Clean

You should include a good dental check and cleaning with each thorough grooming, but you should also have your veterinarian check your Min Pin's teeth at each visit. As with humans, tartar and plaque are an enemy of good canine dental hygiene. Tartar, however, accumulates much more rapidly at the gum line in a dog's mouth than it does on a human tooth. If this tartar is allowed to continue to build up, it can create a gum irritation, which can become an infection, which can ultimately affect a dog's entire health. Severe cases of periodontal disease involve bacterial toxins that are absorbed into the blood supply and that can cause permanent, even fatal, damage to the heart and kidneys. In lesser cases, symptoms of periodontal disease can include loose teeth, loss of appetite, bad-smelling breath, and diarrhea and vomiting.

Regular visits to a canine dentist help keep your dog healthy and happy. Ask your veterinarian what she suggests for continued good dental grooming for your Min Pin. In some dogs, daily brushing and flossing is required; in others, less frequent cleaning is permissible. Inquire also about the proper use of a canine toothbrush and tooth scaler. Never attempt to use a scaler without proper instruction, because you can cause irreparable harm to your dog's teeth with improper use.

The Need to Chew

It's extremely important to give your Min Pin proper items to chew on during the various ages of his life. Puppies and young dogs need something with resistance to chew on while their teeth and jaws are developing. This will help them cut their puppy teeth at the appropriate time, induce growth of the permanent teeth that will already be forming beneath those puppy teeth, and assist in losing the puppy teeth when it's time for the permanent adult teeth to come through the gums. Keeping a Min Pin puppy's teeth "on schedule" is important, because it assures proper jaw development and makes certain that the permanent teeth are settled solidly in the jaws.

If you do have a Min Pin puppy with cropped ears, you'll need to tend to the splints and bandages he needs to wear while they heal and set.

An adult Min Pin also needs to chew. Nature tells him how important it is to chew things for natural tooth cleaning and gum massage and jaw exercise, to say nothing of releasing pent-up doggy tension. We give human babies pacifiers to keep them content, and a doggy chew toy such as a Nylabone can provide that same satisfaction for your Min Pin when his human isn't around for contact. Tooth and jaw development continue until a dog is well past his first birthday, and it can continue far longer if a dog's health has been compromised by injury or disease during the formative period.

Because you don't want your Min Pin puppy cutting his teeth on your new shoes, or your older Min Pin chewing on something he could break or accidentally ingest, it's very important to provide adequate chew toys for your dog throughout his life—and not just for entertainment but for his general health. Be sure to choose items that will be long lasting, good tasting, entertaining, and completely safe from breaking or chipping. The best chew toys are natural bones—I like 2- to 4 inch- (5.1 cm to 10.2 cm) round shin bones—although some smaller bones are considered safe for a dog of a Min Pin's stature.

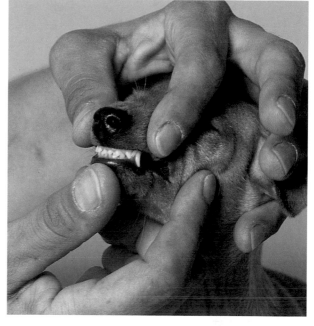

The long-term oral health of your Min Pin should be one of your top concerns. Check the mouth frequently, and learn to brush your dog's teeth.

Some domesticated dogs have teeth far weaker than their wild cousins, so although they still need to chew something, their chew toys may have to be chosen more carefully to avoid too much wear and tear. Some Min Pins have an underbite or wry bite that will cause their teeth to wear incorrectly. If you find that your Min Pin cannot have large, hard, natural bones to chew on, be sure he gets plenty of softer bones such as *uncooked* chicken wings or turkey necks. Doing so will not only satisfy some of his chewing urges but will also provide dental cleansing and good general nutrition. Never give your dog a cooked bone, because the heat process makes the bone more likely to chip and splinter. Cooked bones can create an intestinal blockage and a need for emergency surgery.

Rawhide chews are a good alternative to hard bones as a chew toy for your dog. Just be sure to read the labels and choose rawhide that is processed within the United States, because the quality controls are definitely not adequate in some other countries, which has created health problems in many dogs.

NAIL TRIMMING

Your dog's nails should just touch the ground when he walks. If his nails are clicking on the floor or getting snagged in the carpet, it's time to give him a pedicure. Although nail trimmers look like instruments of torture, in the right hands and with a little bit of knowledge, nail trimming can be totally painless.

Steps for correctly trimming your dog's nails are as follows:

- Use nail trimmers designed for pets. You can ask your vet or groomer what type of trimmers she recommends for your Min Pin. Most will suggest the guillotine type.
- Make sure the clippers are sharp. Dull nail trimmers can split the nail instead of giving a nice sharp cut, which can cause the nail to split upward into the "quick," the portion of the nail that contains blood vessels and nerves. Cutting into the quick can be quite painful for a dog.

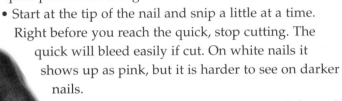

- Start at the tip of the nail and snip a little at a time. Right before you reach the quick, stop cutting. The quick will bleed easily if cut. On white nails it shows up as pink, but it is harder to see on darker nails.
- If you trim too short and the nail begins to bleed, apply pressure and then dab it with styptic powder or a substitute, such as baby powder or white flour. Some people even recommend using granulated sugar or pressing a Min Pin's bleeding nail into a soft bar of soap. Once the bleeding has stopped, be careful not to wipe the clot from the end of the nail.
- If your Min Pin's dewclaws were not removed when he was a puppy, don't forget to trim them when you trim the rest of the nails. Because they never touch the ground, dewclaws grow quickly and can grow into a circle, eventually digging into your dog's skin and causing a potential health problem.
- Trim nails once or twice a month. The quick will lengthen if nails are not trimmed often, so you won't be able to keep the nails as neat and tidy as you might like. Overly long nails can cause traction problems and interfere with your Min Pin's gait.

Bad Breath

No one likes to be around a dog with really bad breath. You may be able to mask the odor with chew toys or charcoal biscuits, but you should still find the root cause of the odor. Although the bad odor may come from something nasty your pet has eaten or licked, it may be caused by something more serious.

The most common cause of halitosis is periodontal disease, which is brought about by the formation of plaque (bacteria). Other causes include metabolic disease (diabetes, uremia); respiratory disease (rhinitis, sinusitis, neoplasia); gastrointestinal problems (megaesophagus, neoplasia, foreign body); dermatological issues (lip fold pyoderma); or nonperiodontal oral disease (orthodontic, pharyngitis, tonsilitis, neoplasia).

As you can see, bad breath isn't just pesky; it can be a sign of a health threat. Have a veterinarian examine your Min Pin thoroughly if his breath is unpleasant. And in the meantime, you can make your pet's breath fresher with this easy (and dogs say tasty) recipe to help neutralize the problem with the aid of activated charcoal, which is readily available at your local pharmacy or market.

No-More-Bad-Breath Biscuits

Preheat oven to 400°F (204°C).

Ingredients:

2 cups brown rice flour

1 tablespoon activated charcoal

3 tablespoons (9.9 ml) canola oil or vegetable oil

1 egg

1/2 cup chopped fresh mint

1/2 cup chopped fresh parsley

2/3 cup (157.7 ml) low-fat milk

Combine the flour and activated charcoal in a small bowl. Add the rest of the ingredients, mixing well after each addition. Using a teaspoon, drop the biscuits about 1 inch (2.5 cm) apart onto a well-greased cookie sheet. Bake the biscuits for 15 to 20 minutes or until golden brown. Cool thoroughly. Store the biscuits in the refrigerator in an airtight container.

Grooming your Min Pin accomplishes much more than just making your pet's coat look nice and keeping him smelling fresh. It should always help you bond and allow you to share quality time that you won't have doing any other activity with your dog. Don't consider grooming your Min Pin as a chore but rather something special you both look forward to. Put on soothing music, make certain that you are both comfortable, and then relax and enjoy your togetherness. You will be content knowing you are caring for your dog, and your Min Pin will be content feeling your love through your touch. Your friendship will flourish!

TRAINING *and* BEHAVIOR
of Your Miniature Pinscher

Why is training important? Surely your Min Pin is so tiny that you can handle him no matter what the situation. How difficult can it be?

No matter what a dog weighs, he can be trouble and get into trouble if he isn't trained properly. For example, not coming when he's called can get him killed if you spot a car or a larger dog coming that he can't see from his low point of view. In addition, if your Min Pin is not able to be easily handled and examined thoroughly, health treatments t may go undetected until they're too late to fix.

We've all seen so-called "armpit piranhas"—small dogs who huddle into the safety of their owners arms, growling and snapping at everyone who approaches. How much happier would this dog's life be if he was happily well adjusted and realized that not everyone is a threat? If you want your Min Pin to be welcome and loved wherever you go, training isn't just important—it's imperative.

Don't use the argument of "my Min Pin just thinks he's a big dog" to make allowances for bad behavior. He knows exactly how big he is. It's because he's as brave as a big dog that he may exhibit dominant behavior. In his mind, the best defense is a good offense. And the only tools at his disposal are his bark and his bite. Don't let him learn to use either to get his way!

LEVELS OF EXCELLENCE IN TRAINING

There are many different levels of dog training. Some owners want to train their Min Pin to do tricks or maybe some simple chores (like fetch the newspaper, slippers, or the leash). Armed with a good book on training, a lot of ideas, and a Min Pin who has a desire to please (which is a trait most Min Pins share), this is an easily attainable goal. Most people are happy to just train their Min Pin to be a responsible family member and then just maintain the basics as time goes by. Almost anyone can manage this type of training!

Other people want to train their Min Pins to actually work with them—hunting (terrier tests are sometimes open to other breeds, although it may take some time to find a group willing to work with you), tracking, therapy (what life wouldn't be brightened with the appearance of a Min Pin's goofy grin?), assistance (Min Pins make great hearing-ear dogs, as very little escapes their attention), or other jobs suited to the Min Pin. This requires a lot more effort on the part of the trainer, and if you're interested, you should be aware that it will likely be necessary to get the support of a

Don't miss the opportunity to train your Min Pin just because he's small enough to pick up and carry around.

professional. It will also require that your Min Pin have the desire to do the job. A dog who is asked to do something he really does not enjoy will soon burn out, and training will become a chore instead of a pleasure for you both.

When you're discussing with Min Pin breeders exactly what you are looking for, be sure that you explain precisely what fields of training interest you. Because the breeder's primary goal will be placing the right Min Pin in the right situation, she needs to know exactly what traits you will expect and want from your dog. Every litter of puppies will have a vast array of temperaments. A sweet, gentle puppy who is happiest cuddling in someone's lap would be the wrong choice for a

family who desires a daily
companion for children or a flyball
or agility prospect. He would be the
perfect choice, however, if you want
a quiet Min Pin who will enjoy
sleeping beneath your desk while
you work or going with you on
rounds at nursing homes or
children's hospitals.

Whether you just want your Min
Pin to learn some basic manners or
whether you find the rapport you
get with your Min Pin during
training so interesting and fulfilling
that you decide to continue training
for competition in dog sports,
joining a local training class will
help you meet people who share
your interest and can help you
achieve your goals. No matter how
far you go with your Min Pin's
training, you will find the time

*As your Miniature
Pinscher's leader, you need
to help show him what to
do in ways that are firm
but kind.*

spent working together a bonding and wonderful experience. Just
remember, until he is sure of what you want him to do, you must
exhibit special patience with your Min Pin. This is not a breed that
will sit back and accept your temper tantrums without letting your
behavior bother them. If your temper starts getting frayed, it is
time to walk away for a while to cool off, and never let your Min
Pin know that he's upset you.

UNDERSTANDING YOUR ROLE AS THE LEADER

There's an old saying that says before you can train a dog, you
must know more than the dog. Although that line usually garners a
laugh from the crowd, it's actually quite true. Obviously, you are
more intelligent than your Min Pin, and you have more education.
But you have to get inside your Min Pin's mind and know how he
thinks before you can be a good trainer. Therefore, from a dog's
point of view, you must know more than the dog and be the alpha
of his pack to be able to teach him.

Choosing a Trainer to Train You and Your Dog

If you decide to go further than the basic family dog training, you should definitely consider hiring a professional dog trainer who is experienced with working with small dogs and with Min Pins in particular. If there's not a professional trainer listed in your telephone book, contact your local kennel club. Most clubs offer basic training classes as fundraisers from time to time, run by members who may not carry the title of "professional" but who certainly have a vast well of experience to draw from. You can also ask almost any veterinarian, groomer, house-sitter, or other dog professional for help in finding a trainer — people in the dog community usually know someone who is a skilled trainer. Check for flyers on the bulletin boards at veterinarians' offices, farm-supply stores, pet-supply stores, and other pet-related markets. If you see someone with a very well-behaved dog, ask her how she trained him.

The first question you should ask a potential trainer is what methods she chooses for training. If she says anything other than "positive reinforcement" or tries to talk you into believing that harsh training methods will work best for your Min Pin, keep looking. Positive reinforcement is quite simply the only training method that will work with a Min Pin. Their stubborn nature will cause them to set their heels and refuse to learn if they are bored or upset by the training. Using too firm a hand will cause them to put their little mental blocks in a row, and no matter how hard you try, you won't be able to knock them down. Someone who is unaccustomed to working with small dogs can also do bodily damage to a tiny Min Pin. Never allow anyone to correct your Min Pin any more harshly than you would. Many otherwise good-natured Min Pins have had their temperament ruined by improper training methods. Don't put your Min Pin's delightful personality at risk! You must make training fun and encourage him to want to do what you ask of him. A good trainer will know this and will work with you to make your Min Pin the absolute best that he can be.

Being alpha means being a leader, and that means exhibiting the kind of behavior you (and especially your Min Pin) expect from a leader. Although Min Pins are very bright and intelligent and willing to work, they are not like Golden Retrievers, whose main goal in life is to please their owners. The independent Min Pin is not a push-button obedience dog, but he can learn good manners and even high-level obedience skills with kind and consistent training. The secret of training is convince him that the good behavior was all his own idea. Min Pins prefer to be the boss of any situation, and they much prefer to do things their own way rather than being told what to do. While they are happy to please an owner they respect, they will be equally happy to call the shots for an owner who does not train with consistency and does not display the bearing and behavior of someone who is always in charge.

The Pack Mentality of a Dog

All dogs are born with a pack mentality, which means that they understand the necessity for someone to be the leader or alpha. Although it's hard to imagine a perky little Min Pin being a close relative to a wolf, he is. And his mind works exactly the same way. Being a "pack" animal means that your Min Pin will strive to reach as high in the pack leadership as possible when he becomes a member of the family "pack" when he comes to your home.

This doesn't mean that he is mean or he doesn't love or respect you. He simply realizes that survival depends on someone being the boss. And if it's not going to be you, it is going to have to be him, and he'll step into the role with his little Min Pin tail happily wagging. One of the most important things you can do for your Min Pin is to teach him early on that *you* are the alpha in his pack. And once you've established that alpha status, it is important to remind him of the fact from time to time throughout his life.

At different stages of your Min Pin's life, especially as he enters puberty, he'll have an innate urge to try to climb up the pack ladder. It is the instinct of any species of animal for the younger to continuously test the older for alpha status, and that goes for every animal, from the wolf to your little Min Pin. For that reason, you should always gently remind your Min Pin exactly where his rung is on the alpha ladder. And that rung must be one rung below yours, as well as all other people. It's okay to allow dogs in a multiple-dog family to establish the pecking order among themselves—in fact, it's a necessity—but they must all realize that they may never question your authority. What you say goes.

If these dogs can sit nicely together for a photo, think what your Min Pin can do for you!

A wolf will test his leader's ability with fang and nail; thankfully, your Min Pin will likely be more subtle. His testing could start with ignoring you when you call him a few times. Then maybe he'll mark your favorite chair with a sprinkling of urine. Or leave fecal "presents" on your bed. Then he'll progress to maybe raising a lip slightly when you reach for his food dish. He won't do anything truly vicious, as that is not in a Min Pin's nature. But he'll come up with a variety of subtle taunts to tell his alpha (you) that he is ready to step into the role of leader. Do not choose to just walk away from the situation. If you ignore even one of those taunts from your Min Pin

without reminding him of his place on the totem pole of your family, you can be creating a problem that can quickly escalate into something serious. Your pet should not fear you, but he must always respect you and know that you are the boss.

Your Min Pin may complain occasionally when he's reminded of his status, but you're doing him a favor. Any dog is truly happiest when he knows what his lot is in life. Your Min Pin will be a happy member of the family when he knows what is expected of him and exactly what the boundaries are for acceptable behavior.

A HIGH-ENERGY PET

Min Pins aren't exactly like any other breed, and their training should be somewhat different from that of other breeds and types of dogs. Yes, all dogs have certain qualities in common—qualities such as the drive to be alpha of their pack. But each breed also has unique qualities that differentiate it from any other breed. Min Pins have evolved into the breed we know and love today through select discrimination and selective breeding for distinctive traits.

Be aware of what makes a Min Pin a Min Pin, and learn to love, rather than try to change, the foibles that make this a unique breed. While they may be exasperating at times, all who love this breed say that the possible problem behaviors are far outweighed by the joy that these prick-eared clowns bring into their lives.

The Min Pin is a very intelligent creature, blessed with a super intelligence that can easily make him the star of an obedience ring or just as easily get him into trouble at home if he isn't watched carefully. A Min Pin can be quite stubborn, but he can still be trained to do almost anything, as long as he wants to learn and continues to finds the lessons interesting. He can be aggressive, but you will rarely find a truly mean or vicious Min Pin (barring one whose circumstances in life created situations where he had to learn to defend himself). The average Min Pin is very energetic, and that high energy level makes it impossible for some people to live with them.

Never let your Min Pin off lead for any reason in an unsecured area. Min Pins are natural explorers. They were blessed with a nose that finds smells to be a good deal more tantalizing than we humans can possibly imagine. And his human's voice becomes small and far away when his nose is trained on a particularly scrumptious scent. Even the best-trained Min Pin will ignore everything around him, including your commands, if he becomes intent on following a visual or scent trail.

TRAINING ESSENTIALS

In addition to maintaining your role as the leader of your dog's pack, there are some other fundamental elements of your training interactions with your Min Pin that must be remembered at all times.

Socializing a Puppy

Right from the start, you'll want to acclimate your puppy to proper conduct around people. Never allow behavior in a puppy that you wouldn't consider acceptable when he's an adult. Ground rules that you've laid at the start of the relationship must be followed throughout your Min Pin's life. Sure, it's cute to hear a puppy's defiant growl when you play tug-of-war with him using a rope toy, and when he wrestles with your hand, you don't find his puppy nips painful—but you must realize that you could be setting the stage for a major problem if your Min Pin continues to think it's perfectly acceptable to growl at humans and bite them. If you don't allow this behavior in the beginning, it won't have a chance to become a problem later.

Part of socializing your Min Pin is exposing him to all sorts of circumstances in a positive way. This can include learning to wear different things, which can come in handy at the holidays.

The same is true for other house rules. If you don't plan to allow your Min Pin on the furniture at any time, be firm and make him stay off it even when he's a cute little cuddly puppy. If he's not always going to sleep in bed with you, don't ever let him. No matter what the situation, if you're not going to accept the behavior later, don't allow it at all.

Socialization: Why Is It Important?

It's just as important for our dogs to learn adequate canine social skills as it is for our children to learn good social skills. A responsible Min Pin owner will take the job of socialization for her dog very seriously. The social skills a puppy learns—and because he grows so rapidly, the window of opportunity is pretty small—will be up to his human. His mother will have taught him his manners when dealing with him and his siblings, but it will up to his human to teach him how he should interact with other humans and the other animals he will come in contact with throughout his life.

Most animal behaviorists agree that the optimum learning opportunity for the socialization of a puppy will occur between the ages of 8 weeks and 14 weeks. Socialization that is begun after that in a puppy who has not received adequate interaction with humans and other animals will be a much longer and frustrating procedure. Not impossible, certainly, but a definite challenge. No matter the puppy or dog's age, the socialization procedure should be much the same.

To correctly socialize your puppy, you should:

- *Introduce your Min Pin to as many humans as you can:* all ages, both sexes, and of as many different races and cultures as possible. Make these meetings positive, and if possible, have treats available for each new person he meets to give to him. This will keep your puppy from reacting negatively to someone he meets who doesn't look or sound exactly like his own human family.
- *Introduce him to children in a totally different manner than older adults.* The puppy should learn not to jump up on them or play too hard with them, and the children should learn to respect the puppy's feelings accordingly. Before a Min Pin can be "good with children" he must be exposed to children who are "good with dogs."
- *Teach your Min Pin to allow humans to be near when he is eating.* If you hand-feed your puppy for a few days and then sit the bowl down and add your puppy's favorite treats to the dish as he eats them, he will quickly learn that having humans near his food bowl is a positive thing. If he reacts aggressively to any contact when he is eating, measures should be taken to correct the behavior immediately. Possessiveness of food can quickly escalate to being a family held hostage by a dog who doesn't "allow" humans to be near anything he considers his.
- *Teach your Min Pin to greet visitors with all four feet on the floor.* This can usually be accomplished if you ignore the puppy

until he is calm. This means no eye contact, no physical contact, and if possible, a complete shunning of him until he behaves.

- *Expose your Min Pin to the noises he is likely to come in contact with throughout his life,* including loud cars, the vacuum cleaner, hair dryer, dishwasher, lawnmower, radio and television, and any other noise that might be startling if an unsuspecting animal hears it. Don't make a big issue of the noise. If your dog appears startled, do not cuddle him or tell him it is "all right." Doing so tells him it is "all right" to be upset or fearful. As soon as your Min Pin recovers from being startled, give him a treat and tell him how brave he was.

- *Introduce your puppy to traffic noises by always making sure that you have a firm hold on his leash,* and start out on a slower street before you progress to a busier part of town. If you live in a rural area, introduce him only to animals you are certain will not hurt him.

- *Introduce your Min Pin to other animals carefully.* Be certain they are not allowed to traumatize him, tease him, or hurt him. And be sure that he is not allowed to terrorize, overwhelm, or harm other animals, either. Most animals will quickly sort out their pecking order, and most will be tolerant of a baby puppy but will give sharper corrections as the puppy gets older. Unless the puppy is likely to be actually harmed or severely traumatized by excessively strong discipline by his peers, allow them to work through the situation on their own.

- *Make sure that your Min Pin learns to spend time alone happily.* A puppy who is never alone will become a dog who will likely suffer separation anxiety and become overly stressed as soon as his owner goes out of sight. Even if your Min Pin whines pitifully when he is left alone, be strong. Give him a fun toy to play with in his crate or sleeping area, and walk out of sight. Stay gone until he quiets down and plays quietly by himself. Then come back into the room, praise him, and give him a treat.

Teach your Min Pin that when people come over he is welcome to say hello, but he should do so with all four feet on the floor.

Miniature Pinschers respond well to praise, affection, and treats.

Remember that it takes proper socialization to become the companion that we all expect our dogs to be. It is your responsibility to provide your Min Pin with the opportunity to learn the things he needs to know to become a well-behaved member of society.

Positive Reinforcement

To get your Min Pin to behave in a way that you find acceptable, you must reward him for doing something right, rather than "punish" him for doing something wrong. A Min Pin won't take kindly to scolding or harsh training. The only thing a dog learns through negative training techniques is to keep away from you.

Training sessions should be short and upbeat. Min Pins become bored easily and can become stubborn if they are repeatedly asked to do something they don't understand. Use lots of positive reinforcement, which can mean simply a lot of vocal praise and lots of pats on the back, or perhaps, knowing that the way to a Min Pin's mind is through his tummy, keep a pocket full of his favorite treats when you are going to attempt to teach him anything new. And always end each training session on a positive note when he has done something correctly. If he's not being successful learning something new, switch back and ask him to do something he does understand. Praise him for doing it correctly, and then consider that training session done for the day. Keep your lessons short and interesting, and make sure that your Min Pin always understands exactly what you're asking him to do.

CRATE TRAINING

In the wild, den animals (such as wolves and wild dogs) don't urinate, defecate, or eat near the place where they sleep to avoid having the scents attract predators to their home. You as a trainer can take advantage of this inherent behavior by giving your Min Pin his very own den. His crate is a place that he can call his own, a place where he will sleep and spend "down time" and know he can always go to avoid being bothered.

Most dogs will be happy to spend time in their crate. It's best to train your Min Pin to quietly stay confined in a crate or other small area where there's nothing easily destructible within reach. Provide him with chews such as Nylabones to play with, as well as a nice soft blanket to scrunch into his favorite position. Most Min Pins are more relaxed when they can hear human voices, so he will likely appreciate it if you leave a radio or the television playing in the background while you're away from home.

Another advantage to the crate is that it's a good accessory for housetraining. Because your Min Pin will be reluctant to soil his den, you can use that fact to help you get him on a schedule for potty breaks. Always keep in mind that even an adult Min Pin has a small bladder, and a Min Pin puppy's is almost miniscule. Never keep your Min Pin in a crate longer than his bladder (and equally small bowel) can manage. As puppies, their sphincter muscles are too undeveloped to hold waste for long periods of time. Except during the night, when they should be sleeping, two hours is usually an acceptable length of time for your Min Pin to be expected to go between outdoor walks. Keeping a puppy or an adult confined to a crate for long periods of time is cruel, not only because his mental state will deteriorate from being away from his humans for so long, but his bowel and bladder can be damaged. Both male and female Min Pins will be much more prone to bladder stones if they are not allowed to empty their bladder on a reasonable schedule. Sooner or later, too, a Min Pin who is kept confined in a crate for too long at a time will begin eliminating in his crate.

HOUSETRAINING

All dogs have certain patterns that they follow throughout their lifetimes regarding their toilet practices. Once you recognize those patterns, you can more effectively allow your dog the chance to eliminate when he needs to.

Getting Into the Outdoors Habit

Whether it's a code word that only you two know, or the more common "go potty" or "go outside," always use the same command each time you go outside for potty breaks to remind your Min Pin that he's there to tend to business and not play. Soon those words will trigger your dog's memory. Once he has eliminated in the chosen place (whether it's outside or inside on newspapers), always give him a reward, and praise him effusively. Let him know that you are absolutely thrilled with his actions. Don't rush him back inside as soon as he finishes the job. Take him for a walk, or play a game of catch with him. Spend some bonding time with him before you go back inside. But don't play with him until he has taken care of business. If he comes to you wanting to play, simply turn your back toward him and give him his command phrase, watching over your shoulder to see if he's responding. Once he has, then it's playtime!

Unless your Min Pin is begging to go back in the house for some reason, chances are that he will prefer spending some time out in the fresh air. Most owners make the mistake of taking their dog outside, letting him eliminate, and then rushing him back indoors. To the adventurous Min Pin who enjoys his time outside, rushing him back inside quickly gives him the message that as soon as he eliminates, his outside time will be over. Therefore, he will take as long as possible to do his business. Oftentimes the owner will see this as a sign that the dog doesn't really have to go to the bathroom, and so she takes the dog back inside, where the dog almost immediately eliminates on the floor. If your Min Pin doesn't eliminate on a trip outside, even after an adequate amount of time,

A crate comes in handy for all sorts of things, from making housetraining and traveling easier to providing a refuge for your dog.

take him inside, spend a little time with him (supervised), or put him inside his crate for a while, and then take him outside again. And after he's done what he's supposed to do outside, play with him, take him on a walk outdoors, or give him a special treat reserved solely for housetraining.

Although it will seem as if he is maybe having more "on purposes" than "accidents," you should never punish your Min Pin for going to the bathroom in the house. The smartest Min Pin in the world has the mentality of a very young human child. And we all know that even older children have toilet accidents from time to time. We can certainly expect no less from our pets. If you catch your Min Pin in the act of eliminating in the house, you should quickly pick him up and take him outside. Don't hit him, or worse yet, rub his nose in it. Rubbing his nose in his mess is cruel and will destroy your dog's trust in you.

Puppy Housetraining

Puppies will need to be given an opportunity to go to the bathroom immediately after they eat, as soon as they wake up, during their play times, first thing in the morning, and last thing at night. Young puppies need to eliminate every couple of hours, while older puppies can go up to four hours between outside trips.

No matter how pitiful he sounds or how much the sound is bothering you, you should confine your Min Pin to his crate at night until he is completely housetrained. Don't give in to his crying and whining. Buy earplugs if you have to, but don't make any contact with him as long as he is being vocal. As soon as your Min Pin realizes that he isn't going to be successful, he'll give up and go to sleep. Some nights it may become a battle of wills, and you'll have to remind yourself who's in charge here. Make sure it's not the puppy!

Always take your Min Pin outside for one last potty trip just before he goes into his crate and the lights dim. (You should probably leave on a nightlight for him and maybe a radio or the television playing softly for company, especially when he's having to adjust to being away from his mother and littermates.) Then wake up as early as possible to take him outside again. If you wake during the middle of the night, you can take him outside then, but don't spend time playing with him. Allow him a chance to use the bathroom, and then put him back in his crate and leave him. Again, don't give in to his pitiful wailings. It's not a good idea to allow him any food or water after about 6:00 p.m., since that would make him have to hold his urine overnight, which is a lot to ask of an untrained puppy.

Housetraining Dogs of all Ages

Some tips and techniques Apply to both puppies and to older dogs. For example, some Min Pins will make obvious signals that they have to go outside. They may whine and walk to the door and stand there looking longingly at the doorknob. Others will circle a few times and look distressed. Still other Min Pins will give more

Min Pins are notorious for having "accidents" on beds and furniture. You may need to come up with some crafty ways to prevent this.

subtle signals that you may have to learn through careful observation. Once you've learned his signal, though, never ignore it. If you do, and an accident occurs, you should apologize to your dog and accept the fact that maybe the problem in his housetraining isn't with him but with you!

Never let your Min Pin have free range of your house until you are satisfied that he is completely housetrained. This can be done with the judicious use of baby gates to confine your dog to the area where you can supervise him.

Make sure that your Min Pin's crate is not too big while he's being housetrained, or he may be tempted to simply eliminate in a far corner of it. If it's too large, you can put a box or other "filler" in the end to take up space, and then remove the box as your Min Pin grows.

Patience is the key to housetraining your Min Pin. If you use a crate responsibly, put your Min Pin on a good feeding and walking schedule, learn to recognize his signals, and clean up thoroughly after every accident, most professional trainers say you should be able to consider your Min Pin housetrained after two to three weeks. Some breeders and owners say that this is a very optimistic estimate, and they suggest lowering your expectations a bit.

Don't let down your guard even when you think the job is completed, however. The most trustworthy Min Pin will fall back into bad habits if you relax his feeding schedule or exercise routines. Housetraining a Min Pin requires commitment on your part, but the more consistent you are in following the basic housetraining procedures, the faster it will go.

Housetraining Hurdles

If your Min Pin is continuing to have accidents in the house after you've followed all the proper training, you should look into what might be the root of the problem. There are many reasons a dog may have accidents in the house. Figure out what is going on and why the problem exists before you go any further with training. A simple thing to check is whether you're simply asking your dog to wait too long between trips outside. If he's getting enough opportunities, it's possible you may have to alter your training methods or wait until a health issue has been corrected before you can see any progress.

The first thing to do if you're continuing to have a housetraining challenge is to have your Min Pin checked out thoroughly by a veterinarian to rule out any medical reasons for the problems. A urinary tract infection or internal parasites will make it almost impossible for your Min Pin to control his bladder or bowels. Both problems are usually quite easily cured, and then you can begin housetraining all over again, hopefully with better success this time around. A Min Pin who has always been trustworthy in the house but suddenly begins having accidents should definitely see his veterinarian to rule out any illnesses or disease.

Some Min Pins will temporarily lose control of their bladders if they become afraid or excited. Remember, this isn't their fault, and they should never be scolded when this occurs. Scolding them will only exacerbate the problem and reinforce their feelings of anxiety and fear.

If a Miniature Pinscher is comfortable in his crate and you know he has recently relieved himself, he should be okay to stay in it for a while.

An unneutered adult Min Pin will oftentimes "mark" his territory by sprinkling small amounts of urine throughout his "territory." This activity can usually be stopped by having him neutered, although it will take time for his hormones to settle down enough to see a real difference in his behavior. If it continues to be a problem and you aren't able to watch him 24 hours a day, you can put a belly band on your male Min Pin. This is a strip of cloth that goes around your male dog's tummy (covering the end of his penis) lined with a woman's sanitary mini-pad. The male may still mark, but the urine will go into

the pad instead of on the furniture or floor. Just remember to change it often, and leave it off as much of the time as possible to avoid infection.

Sometimes males and females will mark through urine or fecal deposits when a newcomer has invaded their territory. This is very common when a new pet, or sometimes even a new human baby, is introduced into the household. Training won't help this issue, but behavior modification—modifying *your* behavior, that is—will make a difference. You'll have to take special care to make sure that your Min Pin knows there's no need for him to feel threatened by the presence of the newcomer.

Some Min Pins may become so anxious at being left alone in the house that they lose control of their bladder and bowels. This separation anxiety can be treated either with proper training or with the use of veterinarian prescribed anti-anxiety medications. These medications can also be of use for dogs who have an inordinate fear of thunderstorms, fireworks, gunfire, or other loud noises. Some Min Pins have such an ingrained fear that at the first sounds, they lose control of their bladder or bowels. If this occurs, remember that it isn't the dog's fault, and he should never be scolded or punished for his fears. You'd hate to be reprimanded or punished because you shrieked when you saw a spider in your bed or a monster in your closet. Your Min Pin's fears are as real to him as your own are to you. Reassure him, and help him build confidence through proper training to work through any behavior issues that interrupt housetraining.

LEASH AND COLLAR TRAINING

A leash will be necessary anytime your Min Pin is outdoors and outside of his fenced area. Making sure he knows how to walk happily on a leash will be one of the best things you can teach your dog.

Introducing Collars and Leashes

Although Min Pins are shown in most performance and conformation events wearing a "show choke" collar, it's never a good idea to put a choke collar on a Min Pin for any sort of training, and certainly not for everyday wear. Most Min Pin puppies can be more easily trained to walk comfortably on a lead if they are wearing a harness instead of a collar. This takes the pressure off the Min Pin's neck. (The pressure exerted by a regular collar can do serious damage.) If you prefer using a collar instead of a harness, you should try a regular buckle collar or perhaps a collar that gives you control with a strap over your Min Pin's nose, rather than putting so much pressure directly on his neck.

Whether you use a special collar or a harness, put it on him first and let him scratch it and worry and fret over it for a few minutes. Give him a treat to take his mind off the collar, and in a few minutes his attention will turn to something else, and he'll soon barely notice that he's wearing anything. Later, attach the leash and

Cleaning Up Accidents

As sure as death and taxes, you'll be cleaning up a lot of accidents until your Min Pin finally gets the housetraining message. Your Min Pin isn't the only one who needs training during this time. You will need to learn exactly how to completely and thoroughly clean up after every accident to avoid repeat occurrences when the smell triggers your dog to make the same mistake again. As long as your pet can smell his personal "mark" in that area, he will continue to return to the scene of the crime.

Not sure exactly where he peed on the carpet? If you can't see the spot with your naked eye, purchase a black light bulb. Turn out all other lights, and the soiled areas will quickly pop into view. Before you turn the regular lights back on, outline the area with nonstaining chalk to be sure that you treat the correct area.

Renting a steam cleaner will probably cross your mind when your carpet becomes soiled. Don't do it! Heat permanently sets the odor by bonding the protein into any man-made fibers. Also, putting vinegar or ammonia (found in many steam cleaning agents) on the stain can actually enhance the odor to your pet and make it even more attractive to him.

The most important thing to do is to clean the area as soon as it is soiled. Use a combination of newspaper and paper towels to soak up urine. The more moisture you can remove before it dries, especially from carpet, the easier it will be to remove the odor. As soon as you discover a spot, place a few layers of paper towels on the wet spot, and then cover that with a few layers of newspaper. (Putting newspaper directly on the spot can cause a stain from the newsprint.) Step on the pile of papers and stand there for a moment, allowing your weight to press the padding to squeeze the moisture from it. Remove all layers of paper and repeat until the paper towel no longer picks up any dampness. Next, using cool water, rinse the area of the accident as well as possible, either picking up the water using the paper towel/newspaper padding effect or using a vacuum cleaner designed to pick up water.

When you clean your carpets, don't use any chemicals in the water; instead, use an enzymatic cleaner designed to break down the protein of pet stains. Once your carpets are well cleaned, use a high-quality pet odor eliminator or neutralizer. Your veterinarian or other dog professional should be able to tell you what products have worked best for them.

If your pet has soiled a washable clothing or bedding item or rug, you should wash it as usual, adding baking soda to the wash cycle. Air-drying the items reduces the chance that the heat of your dryer will set in any lingering odors. Adding an enzymatic cleaner to the wash cycle will help reduce any odors and bacteria as well.

allow him to drag it around. (Obviously you shouldn't do this unless he's closely supervised, in case he gets it tangled around something, especially something that is moving that could drag him.) He will likely chew on it a little bit and perhaps carry it in his mouth "leading himself around." He'll get used to having it tugging at him, and after a bit, he won't fight the resistance.

Walking on a Leash

Once your dog has gotten accustomed to having a leash attached to his collar, you can pick up the end and put a slight pressure on it. For a while, follow your Min Pin wherever he goes, always with only a slight resistance on the leash so that he knows you are attached to him, but you're not forcing him to do anything. After a while, call him to you and have treats when he comes. If he doesn't come, pull slightly to get his attention. Walk away from him, calling and offering a treat. Praise him when he walks where you want him to go.

You should never pull your Min Pin along the floor by his harness or collar. This might not only cause a health problem, but it can create lifetime problems of fear or anxiety and can make him learn to hate or fear being walked on a leash. With patience, he'll learn that the slight resistance isn't a bad thing, and with the promise of treats, he'll happily walk alongside you, focusing on you and your bottomless treat pocket. As with any training session, always end it while he's walking happily. Praise him thoroughly and give him a treat, and then take off his leash and play with him for a while.

Once he's learned to walk happily beside you, you'd think the worst was over, but before you start taking him with

If, despite your best efforts, housetraining isn't working with your Miniature Pinscher, you may want to consult your veterinarian.

you on walks, you should teach him to be calm while you're putting on the collar and leash. Don't allow it to become a puppy rodeo as you struggle to get a collar buckled and leash snapped into place while he jumps and bucks excitedly. Make sure that he learns that if he's not calm enough to let you get the job done, he won't get to walk at all.

Once he learns to be calm while he's being readied for the walk, it's time to teach him that once the collar is in place, it's not rodeo time again. If your dog drags you to the door and then down the street, things are out of control, and it's time for you to exhibit your alpha dog behavior. If your dog begins-out-of control behavior while on lead, simply stand still and gather up his leash until he is pulled up against you. Don't move until he stands quietly at your side. Then begin walking. If he again starts trying to romp and play, stand still again for as long as you need to. Do so as many times as it

This Min Pin is properly outfitted in a collar and leash and is ready to go anywhere.

takes for him to begin walking calmly at your side. You can then give him a little bit of leash at a time so that he can move farther away from you. Each time he gets unruly, pull him back in closer to you, until he learns that if he wants to walk it has to be on your terms, not his. Remember, every time he lunges or pulls you, and you continue walking, you are rewarding him for bad behavior. It is essential that you stand still and refuse to move until he is behaving. This may mean you don't cover much ground on your walks, but in time his little light bulb will go off, and he'll realize that if he walks calmly, he gets to see more territory. Again, patience pays off.

Choosing the Proper Equipment

There are not only a vast number of types and varieties of leashes and collars but also an astounding display of colors, materials, and sizes. It's overwhelming to almost anyone to walk into a well-stocked pet supermarket and see the array of leashes and collars available. While some Min Pins will be able to go through their entire lives with only one leash and collar, most will

With practice (and patience), your Min Pin will learn that the fun part—the walk—only happens when he's calmly in place beside you.

benefit from having an assortment of collars and leashes for whatever "job" they are involved in at the moment. Just remember to choose the right equipment for the right job, and keep your Min Pin's safety foremost in your mind. And as I mentioned earlier, "choke" collars are a poor choice for your dog—they tend to exert a good deal more pressure than is appropriate for a Min Pin.

A Collar's Fit

Probably the most important thing about choosing a collar for your dog is getting one that is the proper size. If your Min Pin is going to be allowed unsupervised outdoors in a fenced area, then you should consider getting a collar with an "easy release" fastener in case he gets tangled in something, to avoid him being choked by his collar. When he's outdoors, even if your Min Pin is microchipped, he should have an identification tag that has your name, address, and phone number (including cell number, since you won't be by your home phone if you're out looking for him) attached to the collar (along with his city license and rabies tags). Although most rescue groups, shelters, and veterinarians can read microchip implants and your lost dog may be returned to you if he is turned in, having a contact name and phone number attached to him could get him returned to you much faster and perhaps avoid having him taken into a shelter at all.

There's a traditional rule of thumb, or rather fingers, to follow when ensuring the proper fit of any type of collar or harness to make sure your Min Pin will be both safe and comfortable. Place two fingers between the Min Pin's neck and the collar. There should be no more and no less room than the width of those two fingers. Too much more space and the collar can easily slip over your Min Pin's ears. Any less space and your Min Pin will be very uncomfortable.

You should check occasionally to make sure the collar still fits correctly, as normal growth of a puppy or weight gain or even thickening hair on an adult can cause the collar to become uncomfortable and can rub the skin raw, creating a health issue.

Collar Materials

Nylon collars are very good for Min Pins who are in the water a lot. Nylon is durable, washable, and comes in a variety of colors, including specialty prints. Nylon can also be embroidered, so you can have your dog's name or a phone number embroidered directly to his collar. Nylon collars can be made from material that is either rolled into a rope shape, or flat.

Leather is as durable as nylon but doesn't come in the variety of colors that nylon does. Leather wears well, however, and will soften from the oils in a dog's coat. Rolled leather collars (rolled into a tight round roll instead of lying flat) will not make an indent on your dog's coat as quickly or as indelibly as nylon, nor will it create static electricity in the coat as it rubs.

Types of Leashes

Measured by the length, as well as the width or circumference of the material, there are as many different types of leashes as there are collars. Choosing the right leash is another major decision. For city walking and training to heel or show in conformation, a shorter leash is usually better. But for some training exercises and for long leisurely walks, a longer leash is suggested. Available in the same materials as collars—chain, leather, and nylon—the type of leash you choose depends on what you will be doing with your Min Pin while he is on lead. Most people choose a leash that will match or complement their dog's collar. Although chain leashes are still available in some places, they are not recommended and are certainly not necessary for a Min Pin. Nylon or leather leashes can be just as sturdy as a chain, and they don't have the annoying clank of chain links to mar your quiet leisurely walks. (They are also easier on your hands.)

If your Min Pin will spend much time on a leash, you should consider purchasing a retractable leash. The nylon lead (some models have a nylon cord, others a flat nylon ribbon) is rolled up and housed in a plastic casing with a grip that you hold in your hand. Much as a fishing reel works, a spring-type function doles out the lead as your dog pulls and then retracts when the pressure is released. You can use the brake function of the leash to "reel" your Min Pin in if he needs to be controlled.

PUPPY KINDERGARTEN

Now that your Min Pin is housetrained and will walk with you on a leash, it's time for him to start kindergarten to learn to interact with other humans and dogs. Puppy kindergarten is not only necessary for your puppy to learn to socialize with other dogs and humans, but it's a place for the two of you to bond into a closer relationship.

Puppy classes consist of socialization and usually some basic obedience training. They also give a professional a chance to watch how you interact with your dog and give you pointers that can help you avoid problems down the road. Undesirable behaviors are much more easily managed when they first start, rather than when they are deeply ingrained. A canine professional can spot potential problems and alert you as to how to deal with them to help make your puppy grow up into a responsible member of your family.

A harness gives you control over your dog and won't pull against his neck should he strain to sniff something.

Your veterinarian or local kennel club can give you information about puppy kindergarten classes in your area.

Choosing a kindergarten for your Min Pin should be undertaken with as much forethought as you would use to choose a day-care facility for your pre-school human child. What your Min Pin learns at kindergarten will stay with him throughout his life. You'll want to be sure he's not only taught the proper things but that he is taught in the proper way. A well-run puppy kindergarten will teach you how to teach your puppy. The instructor will have a gentle voice, and your puppy will likely think she's quite wonderful.

BASIC COMMANDS

You and your dog may work at learning basic commands in puppy kindergarten, you may move on to regular training classes to teach your dog to respond to commands, or you may do all of your basic obedience training on your own. Regardless of the program you adopt, having a Min Pin who responds well to simple commands can be the difference between having a pleasant, well-trained dog and an ill-trained hellion.

When you're training, remember that a dog's attention span is short, especially when he's a puppy, and any distractions will draw his attention away from the job at hand. Keep your training sessions at home short and sweet and full of fun, and try to have several sessions every day. Always end them on a positive note, giving your Min Pin a well-earned treat. Incorporate learning experiences into games and other playtimes so that your dog is learning even when he isn't actually "in school."

The following commands are part of overall obedience training, but if you stop after learning these basics, your dog will be much more easily controlled, and will be happier because he knows he is doing exactly what you ask.

Min Pins respond quite well to tasty treats. Because of their size, they will try to jump up and get them from you. Teach your pup to sit and receive a treat.

Teaching Your Dog to "Come"

The "Come" command may be the most important one you teach your dog. Not only can it save his life by calling him away from danger, but it can help bring him to you in case he is lost and frightened.

To teach the "Come" command, put your Min Pin on a very long lead. Have a pocketful of his favorite treats. Go to the end of

the leash and kneel, calling in a happy voice "Puppy, come" (call him by name). Make sure that you call him in an excited and happy tone of voice. Dogs hear *how* you say something rather than what you say, so you want him to be happy about coming toward you.

Once your Min Pin has heard the command and comprehends what is expected of him when he hears it, continue to take him outside on his long leash, and as soon as he becomes interested in something else, tug on the leash and pull him gently toward you, urging him in a "happy voice." Continue to do this until he is fairly consistent about coming when he's called, and then try the exercise off leash (always inside a fenced enclosure, of course).

It's important to remember to never call your Min Pin to you if the end result will be unpleasant for him. If you want him to come to you for a bath or to take nasty medicines, call him to you and give him a treat, or take time to love him. Then carry on with what you really wanted him for. It's useless to call your Min Pin to come to you for punishment. In his little Min Pin mind that quickly forgot his indiscretion, he is being punished for following your last command—to come. And the next time he hears the command, he will ignore it to avoid the punishment he assumes will follow. Always praise and give treats each time a command is followed.

Teaching Your Dog to "Heel"

Your Min Pin should already be happy on a leash before you attempt to teach him the "Heel" command. With a collar and short leash on your dog, give him the command to "Heel" as you walk. Pull him into position so that his head is level with your leg as you are walking. Keep his leash pulled short, and keep him beside you as you continue to give the command. If he lunges ahead or lags behind, you should gently pull him into position. If he continues to pull away, simply turn and start quietly walking away from him. Keep treats in your pocket, and occasionally give him one to keep him focused on you.

The dog should always walk on your left side, because a dog is shown in both conformation and obedience events from the handler's left side.

Teaching the "Sit" Command

Like any other command, this one is easiest to teach if your Min Pin is particularly fond of treats. Hold a treat just in front of your dog's nose, and slowly pull it back over his head. Most dogs will naturally go into a seated position as they keep their eyes on the treat. Say "sit" and give him the treat while he's still sitting. If he doesn't sit down as he watches the treat, you can gently press his bottom toward the ground, although you shouldn't put much pressure on him. (A Min Pin's skeletal and muscular systems are quite fragile, and too much pressure can cause injury). If he won't stay still while you're working with him, try putting him on a chair, couch, or other, more confined area. Be sure to only give him the treat while he is actually sitting. If you give him the treat after he has moved, he is being praised for doing something other than what you wanted. Don't give your Min Pin a treat just for sitting on his own, either. He should never get a treat for a job well done, unless you have given him the command and he sits after the command is given.

When your dog responds by coming to you when called, be sure you have something to reward him with. Coming to you should be rewarding every single time.

Teaching the "Stand"

Most people don't take the time to teach their Min Pins to "Stand," but it is a very important command for dogs to learn. All dogs should learn to stand quietly for grooming, bathing, examinations by the vet, and if he's a show or performance dog, to stand for examination by a judge. To teach this command, simply hold a treat in front of your dog's face, and say "stand." Only give the treat to him after he has stood quietly for several seconds. Over time, have him stand calmly for longer periods before giving him the treat. At first you may have to physically hold him still and in a standing position, keeping the treat a few inches (cm) in front of his nose so that he stretches to get it. Soon he'll catch on that he can stand and nibble the treat while it's still in your hand, but if he moves, the treat goes away.

Once your Min Pin understands what you want when you ask him to sit, you can practice the request everywhere you go.

The "Down" Position

The "Down" position is usually one of the toughest to teach any dog. In a dog's eyes, this position puts him in a vulnerable posture, both physically and psychologically.

With your Min Pin at the "Heel" or "Sit" position, give the command for "Down" while you make the "Down" signal. (Take your right hand, with the palm down in front of your Min Pin's head, and bring your hand down to the ground.) Pat and praise him for taking the position.

Teaching Your Dog to "Stay"

Put your Min Pin in the "Sit" or "Down" position, and with your hand out, palm facing your dog, give the command to "Stay." Then step right in front of him. Stay there. If he moves, say "no" sharply and put him back into position. When your dog will stay in place for 30 seconds, praise him. (Giving him treats or petting him will likely cause him to break the "Stay.") Once your dog will stay in position with you right in front of him, begin taking a couple of steps away until you are at the end of your leash. Once he will do this well, you can begin walking out of sight (if you are indoors or another securely enclosed area). If he breaks from position, always sharply say "no" and put him back into position. Eventually your Min Pin should learn to stay in whatever position he is told to stay, even with distractions, until he is told that he can move.

No matter what command you are teaching your Min Pin, always end the training session on a positive note, when he has done something correctly. Decide on a phrase to use when the training exercise has finished, so that he knows it is playtime. Remember that a Min Pin is very food oriented, so keep a pocketful of treats to entice him to do his best during each training session. Remember, too, to keep things fun. Min Pins are easily bored, and if the training begins to feel like work to them, they'll set their heels and refuse to cooperate.

MANAGING PROBLEM BEHAVIORS

Remember that problem behaviors are unlikely to be the result of a Min Pin's desire to be naughty. Before you spend a lot of time and money trying to fix problem behaviors, try to establish what is causing them. Learn where they are really rooted so that you can attend to the troublesome behavior without perhaps causing more along the way. It could be that your Min Pin has a medical issue, or perhaps his "problem" behavior is only a problem in your eyes but not in his. It's possible that the "problem" is simply a normal Min Pin behavior that you will have to learn to live with.

Visit a vet at the very beginning of any signs to make sure that they are definitely not medically related. A dog who suddenly forgets his housetraining may be suffering from a bladder or kidney infection or disease. A dog who suddenly becomes fearful or aggressive may not be trying to exhibit alpha behavior but may have a problem that makes him hurt when touched. It is also possible that he is losing his eyesight or hearing and is simply being startled by things that would not faze a hearing or seeing dog. Take your dog to your veterinarian and explain the problems you are having. Have her do a thorough checkup to be sure that some underlying medical condition isn't the culprit.

If you find that there is nothing medically wrong with your Min Pin, perhaps he is just looking for something to do. The Min Pin was bred for centuries to be a companion animal; thus, it is the Min Pin's inherent desire to be with people as much as possible. If you don't plan to keep your Min Pin indoors with you when you are home and either take him with you when you leave or provide him with an array of interesting toys and chewies while you're gone, there is no doubt that you and your pet will suffer. Your possessions will likely suffer as well. Many unwanted behaviors are related to simple neglect. Digging, barking, chewing, and looking for ways to escape are only a few of the ways your Min Pin will find to express his displeasure with his treatment.

This dog is learning to stand in a position that will show him off for a judge in the ring.

As soon as you are certain that your Min Pin is healthy and that the problem behavior is just that—a problem rooted in his behavior—it's time to find a way to fix the problem. As a responsible pet owner, the thought of getting rid of your Min Pin because he has a problem behavior should not be an option. This is your pet. Your buddy. You accepted the responsibility, and that means taking the bad along with the good.

Choosing a Behavior Consultant

Hopefully, your Min Pin's problems won't be anything you can't fix yourself with a little time and a little research into the problem and how to go about retraining. If you find that the problems are greater than you can deal with on your own, you can look for a behavior consultant who can help you come up with a game plan. But how will you find the right person to work with you and your Min Pin?

Most veterinarians and other pet professionals (such as groomers and breeders) will know of behavior consultants or trainers in your area. Call around and find one who meets your needs and who has a personality you think you can work with well. It's imperative that you like the trainer you choose. If you don't enjoy the individual, your Min Pin will pick up on your feelings and will not like or respect the person either, which will be counterproductive to the whole process.

Miniature Pinschers are smart, responsive dogs who take well to training.

Most ethical consultants and trainers will ask for some background of the animal, the problem, and what has been done to date to redirect the behavior at hand. Gathering this basic information gives them a chance to decide if they can help you or if they should refer you to someone more specialized in your specific problem. If they don't ask you for any history but press you to make an appointment, it's probably time to check the next person on the list.

There is currently no organization in the United States that oversees pet behavior specialists, counselors, or trainers. However, the Association of Pet Behavior Counselors (APBC), organized in Britain, does have international membership. To become a member of this group, a trainer or counselor must adhere to humane methods of training (not always the case among some trainers who believe that an animal must fear you to obey you). A good trainer knows that an animal must obey you because he respects and trusts you—not because he is afraid of you. In the US, you might try contacting the Association of Pet Dog Trainers (APDT), which also has clearly defined standards for membership. Members of APDT generally take a stand against training devices that they consider inhumane or cruel, such as electric shock collars, pinch collars, high-frequency startle devices, and the like.

Biting

A Min Pin puppy who is biting you or other family members is simply doing so because he has not yet learned the rules of proper etiquette when playing with humans. He may appear to be acting aggressively, but this does not mean he is going to grow up into an aggressive Min Pin. However, it does show that he has aggressive or alpha tendencies, and you will have to learn how to deal with them and focus them in a positive direction. This is where knowledge of dog body language will come in handy. It may be that your puppy is not biting aggressively but is instead just mouthing you, trying to tell you that his teeth hurt. During the teething age of four to six months, a puppy becomes a chewing machine and should be provided with lots of chew toys to make this time more comfortable for him. Nylabone makes some chews that are suitable for a young Min Pin.

It is very important that you not react with a physical punishment when your puppy mouths you or bites you in play (or in aggression for that matter). If you administer any kind of physical punishment when he bites too hard, he will likely respond in kind. You will be teaching him that he should defend himself whenever someone raises a hand to him, and he is likely to grow up into being a very dangerous, aggressive Min Pin.

Instead of physical punishment, as soon you feel your Min Pin's teeth on your flesh (or clothing), scream as though you are being hurt very badly. This will startle him, and he will release your

Creating Unwanted Conduct

Many times professional trainers and pet behavior consultants will discover that the problem behavior is actually that of the owner, not the dog. Be sure that what you are doing, or asking your dog inadvertently to do, isn't creating more problems than you're solving.

hand. At that time, pat him, tell him he is a good dog, and play a game with him where your hand is not near his mouth. Each time the action occurs, have the same reaction until he realizes that human skin is tender and he can never bite down hard even during play, and especially not in anger. Make sure that all family members follow the same rules when playing with your Min Pin. Don't allow the kids to roughhouse with the puppy or to permit any type of biting, because he will be confused about why it is okay to bite one human and not another.

Never make excuses for an adult Min Pin biting a human. There isn't a good one. Allowing your Min Pin to get away with biting someone—even once—is opening the door to not only possible injuries to visitors (especially children), but in today's litigious society, to a potential lawsuit that can leave you penniless. It's not worth it. No dog should be allowed to bite a human, and even though a Min Pin's bite won't be likely to do life-threatening damage to an adult, it can certainly inflict pain. If you are consistent with your training and socializing, provide adequate leadership (being the alpha of his pack), and acclimate your Min Pin to being touched, the chances are slim that he'll grow up to be a biter. If you begin seeing aggressive tendencies toward humans, it's time to stop the behavior before it's too late.

Dog-to-Dog Aggression

Min Pins show aggression to other dogs for a variety of reasons. Some dogs are simply prone to aggression genetically, while other aggressive dogs were not properly socialized with other animals as puppies. Some Min Pins, usually for reasons also dating back to their puppyhood, feel a need to defend their territory. (Territory could mean their yard, their crate, their home, your bed, or even their human.) Hormones can certainly play a large part in your Min Pin's aggressive behavior. Two unneutered males will be more likely to have a spat than two neutered males. Many times a dog who has always been low in the pecking order in a multiple dog household or environment will develop aggressive tendencies to make up for his feelings of inadequacy. This is where building his confidence in a constructive manner can come into play. Obedience classes are great confidence builders for any Min Pin who needs to feel that he is capable of doing the job that's asked of him.

When dealing with a Min Pin who displays aggressive behavior,

Looking for the Right Trainer

When shopping around for a dog trainer or behavior consultant, there are several questions you should ask anyone under consideration. Inquire as to:

- Where and how long will each individual appointment be? Sixty to 90 minutes is usual for appointments.

- How many sessions will be required? Six weekly meetings are usually sufficient, although severe problems may take longer to resolve, and other needs may become obvious once the training has begun that will extend the timeframe.

- Who must attend? Make sure everyone involved in the problem and correction procedures can attend. If the dog is having problems with specific family members, or one particular "type" of person (male, female, person of a particular ethnic background or specific age group), it will be beneficial if that person can attend with you and your dog.

- What will the training entail? Get "operational descriptions"—will the session be spent sitting and talking, training the dog, or some other activity? Find out exactly why specific things are being taught and how they should help you with your specific problem.

- How much will it cost? Always get a fixed rate up front and preferably in some kind of contract. Some unscrupulous trainers will send a large bill after the fact stating "unforeseen" charges that came up during training. Make sure that you pay one set rate and that any additional charges are agreed upon beforehand.

- Will any special equipment be required? If so, what, and who provides it? If you will be required to purchase any special equipment, get a list of the places it is available. You may want to ask if the trainer can acquire it wholesale or at a reduced cost for you. Ask exactly what other equipment will be used during the training. If she mentions shock collars, spike collars, hanging nooses, hobbles, ultrasonic devices, or other equipment that you have reservations about, be wary. Be sure that the use of any unconventional equipment is absolutely necessary before it is used on your dog, and that it is used only as a last resort. Last resort in this case means that the dog has such severe and deep-seated problem behaviors that if they can't be solved, he will likely have to be euthanized. That should be the only reason that you or any trainer should ever use brute force or any inhumane training device or method on your Min Pin. If you get to this point, get a second opinion from another trainer; don't be swayed by a professional attitude and an "I know more than you do" approach from a trainer or behavior consultant.

- If the problem persists after the program is completed, what happens? Some trainers offer a "money-back" guarantee if they cannot change the dog's behavior. Most don't. Knowing the policy of the trainer will prepare you for the possibility of further classes if your dog persists in his bad behavior.

it is vitally important that you never (even unintentionally) give him any positive reinforcement for the aggression. If your dog growls at another, don't stroke him and say soothingly "It's okay, don't do that." All he will hear is the tone of your voice and the touch of your hand praising him for his behavior. He'll swell up with pride that he protected you from danger, and the problem will worsen instead of diminish. Don't pick him up, either, as that will make him feel helpless, and he will try harder to be a "tough guy" the next time around.

Telling him he's a "good dog" when he shows aggressive behavior will not help make your dog a good watchdog. All it will do is help create a mean dog who will be an insurance liability and who can end up causing problems in your neighborhood that can be costly as well as heartbreaking. Allowing your Min Pin to maintain prolonged eye contact with another dog or thinking it's cute that your little tiny Min Pin barks, snaps, and lunges at the neighbor's Rottweiler can be sounding a death knell for your Min Pin. And it won't be the larger dog's fault when he finally snaps and attacks your Min Pin. It will be yours for allowing the behavior to begin and escalate.

Even allowing your tiny Min Pin to play with a larger dog is an invitation to heartbreak. As careful as the larger dog may be, he could damage your little Min Pin irreparably. And for what reason? To let your Min Pin feel tough? If you love your little dog, you'll know it isn't worth it. You'll keep him away from large dogs who could be a threat. You won't let him think he should be afraid of those dogs, but you also won't let him think he's

Miniature Pinschers who are mouthy need something appropriate to chew on.

tough enough to challenge them, either. You simply won't allow any contact, and he'll learn to accept it, because, after all, you're the boss.

If your Min Pin shows aggressive behavior toward another dog (of any size), it is time to socialize him correctly with other dogs. If you see a dog approaching you, laugh or sing or talk happily so that your Min Pin does not sense any apprehension on your part. If you tighten up the lead to pull him closer to you or start telling him "no" before he has shown any aggression, he will see your action as fear of the other dog, and he will try to spring to your defense. He has no way of knowing that your apprehension comes from not knowing his own intentions.

Each time your Min Pin meets another dog and does not display aggression, praise him and pat him. Do not bring treats into the equation when two dogs are together, especially if one might display territorial aggression. Training your dog to "Sit" or "Down" when he is around other dogs will help enforce your role as alpha and help him realize his role in dog society.

Self-Mutilation

While cats lick themselves frequently to stay clean, dogs rarely do this. If your Min Pin licks himself obsessively to the point that his fur drops and his skin is irritated, have your vet examine him for parasites, foreign objects that might be caught in his hair, or for an allergic reaction to food or medication. If he is not suffering from a physical problem, the licking is an exhibition of stress behavior. This could be manifesting from his relationship with you, with other animals in the household, or because he is unsure of his station in life. Mouthing himself, chewing himself, and excessive licking are the only methods he can employ to relieve tension (much as a nervous human will chew her fingernails or wring her hands).

In this situation, it is very important to build your Min Pin's confidence. Teach him simple commands, and praise him effusively when he does them correctly. Praise him for everything he does well. Spend more time playing with him, and take him for walks. Getting more exercise may also help if the problem manifests itself from stress caused by boredom or loneliness.

Digging

There are many reasons that some Min Pins dig. For some, it is a genetically based behavior left over from when they were bred to hunt vermin in areas where they might have to dig to get to their prey. For others, it's an inherited tendency left over from the time when their ancestors, in the wild, had to dig a den or warming chamber to survive cold winters, or to create a cooling pit beneath the sun-warmed surface dirt in the heat of summer.

It's not always instinct that comes into play, however. A Min Pin who is confined to too small an area outdoors where he quickly becomes bored will dig more than a Min Pin who has a lot of room to explore. Some dogs dig to escape their enclosure. Others dig seemingly for the pure enjoyment of seeing dirt fly. They will move from one area to another, excavating until your yard looks like the surface of the moon with its craters. Some Min Pins dig to hide their bones and toys, sometimes to come back to them later.

Although digging can be a challenging habit to break, it's not impossible. If your Min Pin digs because he is bored, you simply will have to eliminate his motivation to dig by giving him other ways to occupy his time and giving him a place where he is

Min Pins are good-natured dogs who typically get along well with everyone, even at shared feedings.

allowed to dig. Create a sandbox or other area with soft dirt and bury some interesting items (bones, rawhides, treats, and the like) in the soil. At first, bury them near the surface so he can find them easily. Over time, bury them a little deeper so that he will have to work harder to find them. Take him to this area, and give him a command to "Dig," and then praise him when he finds one of the buried treats. Do this several times, and he'll soon get the idea that this is a treasure trove. When he's out of sight, bury more treats, and when you let him outside again, give him the "Dig" command so that he will know that something good awaits him. Soon he'll lose interest in digging in places where there are never any treats awaiting, and he'll limit his digging to this allowed spot.

If you see him digging in an unapproved spot, tell him sternly "No dig," and immediately take him to his area and give him the "Dig" command. Always praise him when he does. You will have to continue to put treats in this area to keep him interested, but in time you can allow more time between placements.

Coprophagia (Stool Eating)

The most disgusting habit (at least to humans) that any dog can take up is eating his own (or other animals') stools. Why do they do this? Most cases of coprophagia appear to be purely behavioral, but there are numerous medical problems that can cause or contribute to coprophagia. Underlying physical causes should first be ruled out before a purely behavioral diagnosis is made.

Your Min Pin may eat his feces if he's not getting enough food or because the nutrition from his food isn't adequate. Check with your veterinarian to see how much food you should be feeding him, and take a label from the food to see if he is getting all the nutrition he needs. Your vet may be able to suggest supplements that will satisfy his cravings. Most inexpensive generic dog foods don't satisfy a dog's nutritional requirements. Generic food passes quickly through his system as well, doing little to supplement as it goes, and it is passed as a stool that looks and smells much like its original form. Usually, feeding a higher quality dog food (you will need to feed less of it, so it evens out in price in the long run) will oftentimes solve a stool-eating problem.

A dog who is scolded or punished severely for having an accident in the house may learn to eat his feces to remove the evidence of his indiscretion. In this case, housetraining him properly should help alleviate the problem.

Coprophagia could result from something you're doing or have done wrong in the past. A Min Pin who is kept confined in a small area for long periods of time may eat his feces in order to keep his sleeping area clean. This is an easy situation to fix, as it only takes giving him a larger area when he is alone. You should also exercise him more frequently and give him greater opportunities to go

Min Pins have a habit of getting into mischief, so be sure to supervise all outdoor activities.

outside so that he won't feel the need to soil his bed in the first place. Keeping a kennel area or dog yard full of feces may cause a fastidious dog to eat his own feces as a way of general housekeeping. Sometimes the smell of so much poop can be enticing to a dog as well, which prompts him to eat it. Keeping your yard clean and picking up feces as soon as they are deposited will alleviate the problem.

Your Min Pin might be like other dogs and want to eat the feces of other animals because they are enticed by the smell and the taste. Sometimes they will want to roll in it as well as eat it. (In the wild, this masked their own scent, so they could more easily sneak up on their prey.)

If all else fails, there are several

additives on the market to sprinkle on your Min Pin's food that will make his poop unappetizing to him and will discourage him from eating it. Once he has lost the habit, you can stop putting it on his food. Some people swear by putting a bit of canned pumpkin in their dog's kibble. Supposedly most dogs don't like the taste of their feces after eating pumpkin, and because pumpkin is full of vitamins and minerals, it's a good food additive anyway, so it certainly can't hurt to try it. Others say that sprinkling meat tenderizer on a dog's kibble can make their feces taste bitter to them. Again, it can't hurt, and if it helps, it's well worth the effort!

Barking

People talk. Dogs bark. And small dogs, for some reason, seem to bark more than larger dogs. It's as simple as that. But when incessant barking becomes a real annoyance, it isn't so simple at all. Excessive barking, as well as barking at inappropriate times, can be corrected, but it's much easier to train a puppy than it is to try to correct an adult dog who has an ingrained habit.

There are many reasons why your Min Pin might get into the habit of uncontrolled barking. Being confined in a space without any interaction from humans or other animals may cause a lonely or bored dog to bark as a way of drawing attention, even negative attention, to himself. Some Min Pins are overly sensitive to every sound and movement around them, and they bark when they are startled.

Min Pins like to dig little nests to make themselves comfy. If they get bored or restless, they may start digging into other things to relieve their stress.

While you can and certainly should lessen the length of the barking sessions and if possible teach your Min Pin to bark in a softer tone of voice (some trainers use the command "Whisper" to get their dogs to bark more quietly, while still not inhibiting their inborn desire to sound an alarm), it is no more reasonable to think you can train your dog to never bark than it is to ask a human to take a permanent vow of silence. It is okay for your Min Pin to bark to sound an alarm; it is simply not permissible for him to continue to bark after he has made the situation known to his humans.

Do not punish your Min Pin for barking. Rather, praise him for not barking. Teach him the command "No Bark," and praise him when he is silent. Whenever your dog is lying around quietly, tell him "No bark" and then immediately "Good dog." When he has barked an alarm, tell him "No bark." When he has stopped, give him the command to "Sit" or "Down," and when he complies, praise him. This tells him what you expect of him after he's barked a warning.

Fear of Loud Noises

The terror some Min Pins feel when they hear a loud noise can usually be traced back to an event from their puppyhood when a traumatic experience occurred at the same time as a loud noise. Sometimes, dogs will "pick up" a fear from their owner. For example, if you show fear at the sound of thunder, your dog may develop the same response to the sound. Fear transference is fairly common from owner to dog, so it is important that you never let your Min Pin sense your fear of anything you do not wish him to fear as well.

Although you should try to avoid altogether any predictable loud noises (such as fireworks on the Fourth of July or New Year's Eve), you should also attempt to desensitize your Min Pin by exposing him to low volume noises while you are creating a pleasurable atmosphere for him, either by giving him a treat, brushing him, or playing with him. This can be a tape of a thunderstorm, rock and roll music, or a movie with a soundtrack that includes a lot of loud noises (like explosions and gunfire) played on low volume. Gradually increase the volume while you continue with your happy time. If you don't show any reaction to the sounds, and good things are happening to him when he is hearing them, soon the fear will no longer manifest itself at all.

If your Min Pin doesn't respond well to the desensitization, it may be necessary to ask your veterinarian for a tranquilizer to give to your dog when you think loud noises might occur that would traumatize him. Because you cannot always anticipate when a surprise thunderstorm will pop up, or a car will backfire, or a child will toss a firecracker in the street, be prepared to work with your Min Pin to help him through his fears. When the noise occurs, act happy and unconcerned. If your dog sees that you are not

The best way to keep your dog from eating feces in the yard is to monitor his time outside and diligently pick up after him.

frightened, it can help him realize his fears are unfounded. Always be sure your dog has a safe place—his own crate, under your bed, or in a closet—to run to when he is afraid.

Jumping Up

Puppies jump up on us as a way of greeting and expressing their joy at seeing us, and we don't mind because they are little and cute. However, the same action from an adult Min Pin that has the end result of tearing or dirtying our stockings or clothes becomes a problem. The best way to avoid jumping up as an adult is to nip this conduct in the bud when your dog is a puppy. (This rule applies to wherever you don't want your dog; if you don't want your adult Min Pin to get on the furniture, don't hold him there when he's a puppy. If he won't be allowed in your bed later, don't take him there when he's a baby.)

If you find yourself with an older Min Pin whom you need to retrain, just remember to get down to his level when you first see him after being away, which is usually when he will want to jump on you the most. You must always be consistent so that you don't confuse him. Don't scold him for jumping one day and then pat your chest urging him to "give you a hug" or jump up into your arms the next. Make the decision of what you expect from him, and make sure that he knows what that is.

The key to stopping this behavior is to shout "off" loudly when he jumps up on people or furniture. You want to startle him so that he pays attention immediately. Tell him to "sit," and then praise him and give him a treat when he does. He should quickly learn that when he approaches you or others, he should sit quietly and wait for attention from you.

BODY LANGUAGE

Even though your Min Pin can't speak with words, once you become tuned in to him, you will be able to read his body language as well as you can understand human words. Be aware that he is also quite capable of reading *your* body language. When training, for example, stand up straight and let your dog know that you are confident. Learning to understand what your Min Pin is saying with his body is important, not only to get to know your own dog better but to predict what strange dogs will do. There is no real guideline to reading body language. It takes experience watching your own dog and others. Go to a place where you can watch dogs interacting and watch their different body parts: lips, hair, tail, ears, eyes, as well as their overall posture.

This Min Pin is focused on getting whatever it is he has his attention on. If his fixed attention doesn't get results, he will probably bark.

Soon you will be able to predict how body postures and other signals are portents of what he is thinking.

- **Confidence:** A confident Min Pin will have an erect stance, standing and walking tall but relaxed, tail up and wagging, and will give you a direct look. (Usually, his eyes will have a somewhat constricted pupil.)
- **Lack of Confidence:** A Min Pin who is afraid or concerned will carry himself with a lowered stance with his tail down, sometimes even tucked, depending on the level of his fear or concern about his situation. His tail may wag, but it will likely be a quick, frenetic wagging, not the lazier wag of a happy dog. He will likely not look at you directly and may even turn his head away, showing you the whites of his eye (often with a somewhat dilated pupil). Many will curl up or try to make themselves appear as small and insignificant as possible. You should never reach out to a Min Pin who is showing fear. He will likely only back away and growl; however, if he is stressed enough, he could snap at you. Instead, use your own body language to show him you

mean him no harm. Turn sideways, look away, and yawn until he appears more relaxed, at which time you can hold out your hand to him. Don't put your hand into his space, but leave it in a neutral area between you, allowing him to move toward you to sniff it.

- **Fear:** A fearful dog will flatten his ears, part of the attempt to make himself appear smaller and to keep them out of harm's way. He will likely also put his tail between his legs, covering the scent glands to mask his identity.
- **Stress:** Your Min Pin can get stressed from something as simple as being left alone for the first time or being asked to learn a new task. Some of the signals that your Min Pin is becoming stressed are shaking, submissive urination, ears back, dilated pupils, rapid panting (with corners of mouth pulled back), sweating through paw pads, yawning, rapidly blinking eyes (eyes open wider than usual), and placing the tail down (sometimes tucked tightly).
- **Humping or Mounting:** Mounting or humping are used both as aggressive behaviors and in play. You will have to watch for other body postures to decide what the dog in question is trying to say by his action.

- **Anger, Aggression, or Arousal:** An angry Min Pin will usually raise his "hackles" (the area over the shoulders, sometimes reaching back toward the base of the tail). This doesn't always mean the dog will be aggressive, but it means that he has gone into a stage of "red alert" and is prepared to go to battle at the slightest hint of danger. If a dog has stiff legs and a stiff body, his tail stuck straight out from his body, a lowered head with ears "pinned" against his head, eyes narrowed and fixed intently, and lips drawn into a snarl with raised hackles, he has gone from red alert into war mode. Be wary and do not attempt to touch this dog, and be careful not to make any sudden movements.
- **Dominance:** Any dog who stands over another dog, puts his paws or his head over another dog's back, or looks aloof when another dog licks at his lips is showing his dominance over the other dog. He will usually stare the other dog in the eye.
- **Submission:** A submissive dog will keep his head and body lower than the dominant dog, calmly accepting the other dog's dominant gestures. He might lick at another dog's mouth, not

meet the other dog's (or human's) eye, and will oftentimes roll over on his back and expose his tender underbelly in a gesture saying "I am not going to fight you." Oftentimes the severely submissive dog will urinate, whether out of fear of the other dog or as some sort of canine "uncle."

- **Play Gestures:** The classic "tail and butt in the air" while the front legs are lowered, also called a "play bow," is a dog's invitation to play. Many dogs will "grin," and their eyes will look open and relaxed. Puppies will sometimes paw the air like a kitten when they are trying to induce their littermates into puppy games. Among dogs, these actions seem to be some sort of indicator that anything that follows should not be taken as a serious attack upon the other dog(s). A dog's "play bark" will usually be higher pitched than that dog's "fear bark" or "warning bark."

Min Pins are athletic, energetic dogs for whom jumping just comes naturally.

Remember that dog behavior differs greatly from human behavior. The general rule should be to let dogs be dogs and sort out for themselves what is appropriate and what is not. Butt sniffing, rough playing, barking in each other's ears, humping, and other normal dog actions wouldn't go over well at a human soiree, but they are perfectly acceptable, even welcomed, in polite dog society.

When dogs (or humans) misunderstand dog body language, trouble is likely to occur. The breeds of dog that look most like their feral ancestors (German Shepherds, for instance) will be able to show much clearer body language. Those that are far removed from this wolfish appearance, such as the Min Pin, are more likely to be misunderstood.

If you see that your Min Pin is doing something that is not considered acceptable dog behavior, you should immediately rectify the situation. Call your dog away, and interest him in another activity.

ADVANCED TRAINING
and ACTIVITIES
With Your Miniature Pinscher

I t's very important to occasionally stop and remember why you purchased a dog in the first place—for companionship. Throughout this book, you will see your Min Pin being referred to as a "pet" no matter what other activities he enjoys on the side. He should always be your "pet" before he is anything else. Don't let points, ribbons, titles, or awards become so important to you that you forget that this perky, bouncy little guy is a living, breathing creature, dependent on you, his owner, not only for food and shelter but for love and companionship. He should always be your "pet" first and a "therapy," "show," or "performance" dog second.

CANINE GOOD CITIZEN (CGC) PROGRAM

Having his Good Citizenship Certificate means that your Min Pin will be welcome pretty much anywhere you go with him. A Good Citizenship Certificate is awarded under rules established by the American Kennel Club. The program is open to all breeds of dog, regardless of registration, and to mixed breeds. It is a two-part program designed to:

1. Teach responsible dog ownership to owners.
2. Certify dogs who have the training and demeanor to be reliable, well-behaved members of their families and communities.

The CGC test is not a competition, and dogs are not given a score but instead are graded on a "Pass" to "Needs More Training" scale. The purpose of the CGC program is not to provide an avenue of competition but simply to ensure that your dog can be a respected

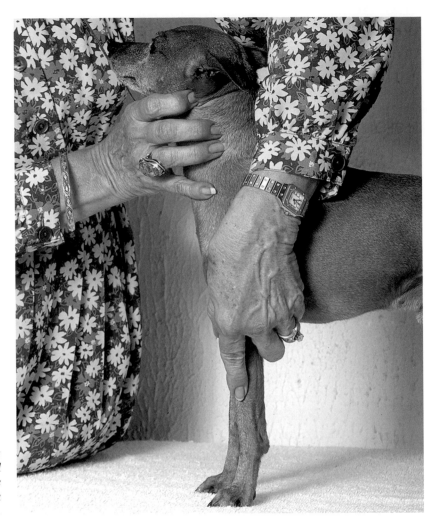

Allowing a friendly stranger to inspect and groom him is part of the behavior expected of a Canine Good Citizen.

member of the community because he is trained to act mannerly in the home, in public places, and in the presence of other dogs. Dogs who pass all ten items of the test receive a certificate from the American Kennel Club, tangible proof that the dog is indeed a "good citizen." (This certificate will be of importance should you decide to use your dog as a therapy dog at hospitals, nursing homes, and retirement facilities.)

There are some aspects of the test over which your Min Pin will have no control. These will be up to you—he must appear for the test well groomed and clean and wearing an appropriate collar or harness (not a pinch, electronic, or training collar). You should bring a brush along for the examiner to use to demonstrate the dog's tolerance for being handled by a stranger. You should also have proof of vaccinations, including rabies and DHLPP. (Ask your veterinarian for a printed copy of your records).

Other than having your dog properly groomed and being prepared with your "props" and paperwork, the rest is up to your dog. Your job will have been done long beforehand as you patiently taught him what being a good citizen was all about. The ten parts of the Canine Good Citizen test are:

- **Test 1: Accepting a Friendly Stranger.** An examiner will approach you and your Min Pin and talk to you in a friendly manner, possibly shaking hands or making some sort of body contact. Your Min Pin cannot show any aggression or defensive posturing.
- **Test 2: Sitting Politely for Petting.** The dog must allow the examiner to pet him while the examiner is talking to you in a friendly manner. Your Min Pin cannot show aggression, overexuberance or enthusiasm, or defensive posturing.
- **Test 3: Appearance and Grooming.** Your Min Pin must allow a stranger to brush and examine him.
- **Test 4: Out for a Walk.** This demonstrates your Min Pin's ability to be easily controlled while walking on a loose lead. It doesn't matter which side you choose to walk your dog, although traditionally the dog walks on the handler's left side.
- **Test 5: Walking Through a Crowd.** This test will demonstrate your Min Pin's ability to move about politely in pedestrian traffic and be easily kept under control in public places while on lead. The people he meets will be doing all the things people might do in a public place— opening umbrellas, walking on crutches, swinging a cane, and crossing suddenly in front of you and your dog. Your Min Pin should not pull at the leash, jump at the people, or show excitement, fear, or aggression.
- **Test 6: Sit and Down on Command/ Staying in Place.** This test will demonstrate that your Min Pin has had basic obedience training and will respond to your commands to "Sit" and "Down" and will remain in the place he's told to stay. A dog's willingness to respond to these commands is not only convenient, but sometimes it's a necessity—both in unusual situations and in normal life routines. The examiner will ask you to have your Min Pin "Sit" and then "Down" on

command. You will be asked to tell the dog to "stay," and then you will step away from the dog and call him to you. The dog should stay until called and come when called. Unlike formal obedience competition, repeating a command is allowed.

- **Test 7: Coming When Called.** This test demonstrates that your Min Pin will come when called. Coming when called is extremely important, because it can save your dog's life.
- **Test 8: Reaction to Another Dog.** This test shows that your Min Pin can behave politely around other dogs. Most dogs will come in contact with other dogs and animals at some point in their lives, sometimes on a routine basis. And if a dog is a show or performance dog, the social skills needed to pass this part of the test are crucial.
- **Test 9: Reaction to Distractions.** This test demonstrates that your Min Pin is confident when faced with common distracting situations. These situations can be something as mundane as someone walking toward him to someone coming toward him swinging a cane or opening and closing an umbrella. The distraction could also be another dog or a child.
- **Test 10: Supervised Separation.** The supervised separation test shows your Min Pin's ability to maintain his training and good manners when left with a trusted person or stranger. Your dog must remain calm if you leave him briefly. The examiner will direct you to secure the dog to some object and

Being able to hold a "Sit" while being distracted shows that your Min Pin understands what's being asked of him.

Sports and Safety

Although you and your Min Pin will both be healthier, happier individuals if you spend time together doing some sort of performance activity, remember to keep safety issues first and foremost in your plans. Obedience, agility, and tracking, as well as other canine sports, can all put wear and tear on a dog's body. Before you and your dog undertake any strenuous new activities, check with your vet (as well as your own doctor) to be sure that no one's health will be compromised by the increased activity. Start out slowly, and don't overdo it. Follow all the rules and regulations of any organized event or training classes you attend, and avoid any circumstances that could lead to danger. Never push your Min Pin to complete a course or trial if he appears to be ill or limping. A canine athlete is as likely to have a sports injury as any human athlete, and your overexerted Min Pin can suffer serious, even permanent, physical damage. Make sure that you are prepared to take care of him in any emergency, and be aware of potential problems and safety issues in any sport in which you choose to train and work.

Before engaging in any kind of organized competition, be confident that your Min Pin is very comfortable around crowds and other dogs. You must be able to control your dog at all times. Your ability to do so not only eliminates the potential problem of his being attacked by a larger dog but also the chance of him being accused of either provoking a large dog to attack or of him going after another smaller dog in case of a squabble.

then go out of the dog's sight. Your Min Pin may move around and show interest in his surroundings, but he must not whine, bark, pull, or otherwise show distress. An important point to note is that the dog is not left alone but is being left under the indirect supervision of a stranger. You can interact with the examiner before you leave, so your Min Pin will be aware that he is not being abandoned and that you trust this stranger.

Recovering his poise after excitement is also part of the test. You will be asked to play with your dog and get him to play with you. You should then be able to immediately calm him down.

Preparing for and taking the Canine Good Citizen test is a great way to develop your Min Pin's obedience and social interaction abilities. Even if you have no plans to do any kind of formal competition or service with your dog, working with him to pass the test is excellent basic training.

THERAPY AND SERVICE DOGS

Once your Min Pin has received his Canine Good Citizenship certification, he will be welcomed into almost any hospital, nursing home, school, and child and adult care facility. Now your dog is ready to visit with the sick, elderly, and rehabilitation patients and to provide canine education programs to children.

Your Min Pin doesn't have to have a certificate to be welcome at most places, but he does have to prove himself capable of handling the situation. He cannot do that without some background work on your part. Not only is it necessary that he has the right temperament to be trustworthy around the elderly, young, and infirm, but he must have learned some basic manners. He should also have been exposed to a great number of unique situations that will prepare him for the unusual things that he may encounter on his rounds as a therapy dog. If you can't find a training class for therapy dogs in your area, you can do much of the training yourself. Basic obedience (with an emphasis on the "Sit," "Stay" and "Down/Stay" commands) and field trips with your dog to public places, especially nursing homes and places with lots of children, will help turn him into a dog who will bring smiles to the faces of many.

Some of the places you might consider taking your therapy dog in training include:

- **Shopping centers or malls:** At the mall, your dog will encounter shopping carts, escalators, elevators, people carrying large bags, umbrellas, and canes.
- **Downtown streets:** In busy areas with lots of cars and pedestrians, your Min Pin can get used to strange noises and the hustle and bustle of a lot of strangers.
- **Hospitals and nursing homes:** Try some test-runs at hospitals and nursing facilities to visit adult patients who understand they are serving as part of the dog's training. This will allow the dog to come in contact with people in wheelchairs, using walkers and canes, and walking with portable IVs.

Once your Min Pin has learned some basic commands and become accustomed to being with strangers, around a variety of odors, and among the various equipment commonly found in medical facilities, he will be ready to join you for some of the most heartwarming and rewarding experiences of your lives.

May I Be of Service?

Many people are confused about the difference between therapy dogs and service dogs. Although both provide a great service to the

Their small size makes well-mannered Min Pins wonderful therapy dogs.

people whose lives they touch, they do so in different capacities.

Therapy Dogs

A therapy dog is one who accompanies his owner or other volunteer to hospitals, nursing homes, and other facilities in order to provide companionship and cheer. Not only do therapy dogs brighten the day of those who are sick or infirm, but they also bring a smile to the faces of visitors and staff. Some patients and nursing home residents come to look forward to the visits with great anticipation. If you have time to spend—for example, one afternoon a week— I assure you that you'll find the experience very rewarding for both yourself and your dog. To ensure that the dog will be well behaved, volunteers must provide paperwork and receive validation and an invitation before the dog is allowed into some public facilities.

Service Dogs

Service dogs are specially trained to serve one owner who needs their help to enable them to live independent lives. Service dogs include guide (or leader) dogs for the blind; hearing dogs who alert

How Are Dogs Judged?

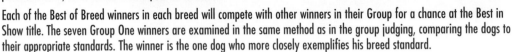

When showing in conformation, each dog is evaluated as to how well he reflects the characteristics set forth in the breed standard. He is not judged against the looks of the other dogs. For example, competitors in the Toy group vary from the hairy Maltese to the hairless Chinese Crested. Comparing any two dogs of a different breed is like comparing apples and oranges, so the judge compares the Min Pin to his ideal and the Maltese to his ideal and so forth. Is the apple a better apple than the orange is an orange, so to speak? The winner will be the dog who, in the opinion of this day's judge, best exemplifies his standard for his breed. If your Min Pin is considered to be the best representative of the breed (Best of Breed) at a particular show, he continues to compete at that show.

Each of the Best of Breed winners in each breed will compete with other winners in their Group for a chance at the Best in Show title. The seven Group One winners are examined in the same method as in the group judging, comparing the dogs to their appropriate standards. The winner is the one dog who more closely exemplifies his breed standard.

their owners to sounds; mobility assistance dogs who may either pull a wheelchair or provide support for a person; seizure alert dogs who alert their owners to oncoming seizures; and other dogs specifically trained to provide various types of support for their owners. A service dog is entitled to go into any place that his owner goes.

THE SHOW MIN PIN

Although not always the "showiest" breed at a dog show (when compared to the elaborately groomed Poodles and fluffed and primped long-haired toy breeds), any well-bred, outgoing, well-trained, and well-conditioned Min Pin who loves the show ring can always be a contender for Group and Best in Show placements. No dog can be shown in the conformation ring in either the US or Great Britain for points until he is six months old, but you should be able to find some puppy matches nearby for good experience before that time. Puppy matches are run in the same style as a "real show" but in a much more relaxed and informal setting.

No matter how excited you are about showing your Min Pin, it is probably best to wait until he is at about two years old to show him frequently. Most Min Pins don't truly "come into their own" until that age. With physical maturity also comes the mental maturity necessary for a show dog to compete day after day, week after week. Many a lovely Min Pin puppy with the promise of turning into an equally lovely Min Pin adult has been ruined by being pushed too hard and too fast into a show career.

A Conformation Mentor

Finding a good mentor for entry into the dog show world can be critical to your dog's success. There is nothing that can get you farther and faster in the dog world than having an established person in the breed take you under her wing. No professional training can compare with a dedicated breeder/exhibitor who allows you to pick her brain for information, sharing her wisdom acquired through many years of making mistakes and witnessing those that others have made.

You may have the "best" Min Pin in the country and may be lucky enough to enjoy some initial successes, but your long-term involvement in showing your dog will depend largely on your relationships with others in the sport. If you chose your breeder carefully in the beginning, in all likelihood this breeder will be your mentor. After all, she knows the characteristics of her particular bloodline, and she knows the tricks and tips to getting your dog into proper condition—both his coat and his conduct. Your dog's breeder, moreover, will have her own reason for wanting your Min Pin to do well in the ring. As the breeder of your Min Pin, her

The dog show world is exciting and competitive. If you think that it's for you, find a mentor who can help you learn all about it.

name will be entered in every show catalog at every show at which your dog is entered. If you and your dog look good, she, in turn, looks good.

Your mentor will be the one who receives your excited calls the first time your dog walks out of the ring with a purple ribbon. She'll also be the one whose shoulders get wet from the tears of happiness and sadness you'll shed over the years with your dog. She'll have carefully bred your Min Pin to conform to the AKC standard for the breed. However, even if you have a Min Pin who is the epitome of what the breed standard describes, if he is not a good showman, it will be hard to finish his championship.

The Qualities of a Champion

A true show dog is born, not created. From his first toddling steps in the whelping box, he will have a "look at me" attitude that his littermates lack. Without this spark, this "something special," even the best Min Pin will often be beaten by the lesser dog who carries himself like a showman.

To become a US champion, a dog of any breed must win 15 points awarded by AKC judges at AKC-sanctioned dog shows. Computing points is complicated, as breed points differ not only

What (and What Not) to Wear: Conformation

We all have seen the shows on television aimed to outfit normal people for normal, everyday lives. But what about the dog person who's looking to fill her closet? What outfits and clothing are considered proper for all the different events you can share with your dog?

No matter what the event, unless it's perhaps the Best in Show ring at Westminster, it is always best to dress conservatively. No dangly or jingly jewelry, no glitter, and nothing else that might distract or detract from your dog. You should always wear comfortable shoes with a nonskid sole. Make certain the sole is not soft rubber that can grip ring mats too well and cause a tumble. Any outfit you choose should either have pockets for bait and show paraphernalia, or you should purchase a clip- or pin-on bait pouch and select clothing that has a good attachment point.

When handling your dog in the show ring, remember that you are a background for your dog. You're not the one who should catch the judge's eye, but you should create a vignette with your dog that will bring his eyes to you both. As for the level of formality in dress, most people wear outfits that would double as appropriate clothing for a job interview. If you are showing only one dog, you should choose a color of outfit that will coordinate well with him but not hide him. Jewel tones work really well with almost all colors of dog. Black or white make excellent backgrounds for the opposite color of dog. Prints should be chosen carefully, because they can direct attention away from your dog. Don't choose a color that is very similar to that of your pet, as this can make him appear to fade away.

from breed to breed but from one section of the country to another. The more dogs of your breed and sex that you compete and win against, the more points you win along with that coveted purple ribbon. The most points any dog can win at one show are five points. Wins of 3, 4, or 5 points are called "majors," and among your 15 points must be wins at two "major" entries. The rest of the points can be made up of either more majors (if you're really lucky, and you have a superior Min Pin) or single points won at smaller entry shows.

Note that only unspayed bitches and intact males may compete at AKC conformation shows. This rule harkens back to the original purpose of dog shows, which was to select those dogs who would produce the best offspring. Many exhibitors think this rule is outdated and should be abolished or at least changed to allow sterilization in some circumstances. Unless you will be showing your Min Pin in conformation or are planning to engage in a well planned breeding program, you should definitely have your dog altered.

It's a good idea to go to dog shows simply to observe before going in the ring yourself.

To become a Show Champion in Great Britain, the dogs who win each class compete for Challenge Certificates (C.C.'s), dogs and bitches separately. Once you have three C.C.'s from three separate judges, your dog is considered a Champion. As in the US, after the C.C.'s have been awarded, the Best of Breed winners from each group (gundogs, working, hounds, and others) are judged to find Best of Group. These are then judged for Best in Show.

Entering a Show

Once your Min Pin is old enough, adequately trained, and in his best condition, and you're both working together well as a team, it's time to enter your first dog show. Most dog shows in both the US and Great Britain close their entries at least two weeks before the actual date of a show. Locate the superintendent of the dog shows in your area, and get on her mailing list for upcoming shows. There is always a listing of upcoming US shows in the *AKC Gazette.*

To enter a show, an entry form must be filled in giving the details of the dog (including sire, dam, breeder, birth date, and address of owner), as well as for the class in which the entry is being made. This must be mailed, along with the appropriate fee (which varies from show to show and class to class entry), to the show secretary, and it must be received before the deadline given for entries. Once the secretary has received all entries and the deadline has passed, a catalog of all the entries is compiled and printed and will be available on the day of the show.

If you want to handle your Min Pin in the ring yourself, it's a good idea to take your dog to some handling classes. Not only will your Min Pin benefit from the socialization experience, but the handling skills you'll learn will build your confidence in the ring. You'll learn not only ring protocol but also show terminology, dress codes, and how to present your Min Pin to his best advantage.

If you decide you don't want to show your Min Pin yourself, there are professional handlers in almost every area of the country.

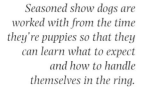

Seasoned show dogs are worked with from the time they're puppies so that they can learn what to expect and how to handle themselves in the ring.

Conformation Showing in the US and in England

The differences in British- and American-bred dogs are subtle, but they may make it difficult for a particular dog to achieve a show championship title in a country other than that of his origin. American judges tend to place more emphasis on the dog's markings and the presentation of the dog. In other words, more emphasis is placed on the general appearance of the team of dog and handler.

The British judges seem to look more closely at a dog's body proportions so as to give a more correct movement, and they focus entirely on the dog, with little thought as to the handler's appearance. British judges usually insist that handlers move their dogs more slowly than do American judges, which sometimes makes improper movement more readily visible. Breeders in both countries are quick to say that they admire the depth and quality of breed type in the other nation's breeding programs. In fact, many breeders import dogs from the other country to improve their own breeding program.

You can either turn your dog over to them until he is finished or take him from show to show, handing him off ringside. (Most handlers prefer to have the dog in their possession for at least a week or so before a show for grooming and training preparation.) If you decide to hire a handler, be certain to choose someone who is well known for her love and attention for the dogs in her care. Many handlers become so popular that they have large "strings" of dogs who go with them to each show, making it less likely that your dog will get any one-on-one attention during the time he's being shown, other than for grooming and training. Make certain that the handler you choose believes in letting dogs be dogs and allows them adequate exercise and fun time. It's also important that the handler you choose be someone who's used to showing small dogs, and with some luck, you'll find someone who is particularly skilled at showing Min Pins.

Although dog shows should be fun days, remember to watch your Min Pin closely at all times. Bad experiences, such as being jumped on by larger, snarling dogs can wreck a show dog's career before it starts. Even though most Min Pins seem to think they can take on any adversary no matter his size, the disadvantage of being startled during a time when he is feeling stress from his owner can make it a traumatic event for your little guy. Make sure your own dog is a good sport as well and knows how to be a good citizen. Remember that his "cute" attempts to go after larger dogs may not be so funny if they provoke a big dog to fight. Even a good handler can be caught unaware, and your Min Pin could be injured or even killed if a severe altercation suddenly occurred. Always carry your

Min Pin through crowded aisles, and don't risk him becoming bait for a big dog with an attitude.

Preparing Your Min Pin for the Ring

Your Min Pin will need to learn basic manners as well as some basic obedience before you can expect him to consistently win. He must:

Mastering the fundamental commands both on and off leash are necessary to compete in obedience.

- Learn to walk quietly at your side in and out of a ring.
- Be willing to allow you to place his feet and his head while he is being "stacked" for examination and to hold whatever position you place him in until you tell him it is okay to move.
- Stand quietly on the ground and on a table while a judge examines him thoroughly.
- Learn to tolerate his peers without showing any aggression or even play tendencies.
- Learn to trot at whatever speed you ask him, matching his speed to yours, on a loose lead or with pressure on the leash to ask him to hold his head higher.
- Learn what "No sniff" means. To show well, a dog must keep his nose off the ground in the ring, ignoring the tantalizing aromas that surround him.
- Learn to keep all four feet on the ground, even though your pocket will reek of some of his favorite treats.

A conformation dog isn't just bred and trained; he must be conditioned as well. The most well-bred Min Pin who is trained and handled to perfection won't stand a chance against an equal competitor who has been excellently conditioned. For some Min Pins, conditioning may require a strict exercise and diet regimen. For others, just brisk walks with their owner may do the trick. Some handlers don't have the time to personally walk their "string" of dogs, so they condition them using a treadmill. Whatever method you use, be careful not to overdo it. Nicely developed muscles are good in the right amount and place, but your Min Pin shouldn't look like an overdone canine version of a bodybuilding contest winner. He should have the proper muscle tone and weight for his breed and sex. His skin and hair should be in good condition as well. Getting your Min Pin into shape may take a while to achieve, but it can be easily maintained with the proper diet and bathing regimen.

The tunnel is just one of the many obstacles a dog must navigate on an agility course.

OBEDIENCE TRIALS

No one who has shared his or her life with a Min Pin will ever associate the word "obedient" with the breed. While some breeds were selectively bred for their willingness to please their owners no matter what, the Min Pin definitely isn't one of them. Bred for generations to be tenacious ratters, with an eye only toward catching their quarry, they become single-minded when focused on a goal. This gene is the same one that will cause a Min Pin to totally ignore his owner's voice if he is intent upon following a good smell, tracking down a sound, or chasing after some fast-moving prey. Pleasing themselves is always their foremost concern, with pleasing their owners usually coming in a firm second.

Although there are some wonderful working Min Pins who can give the other breeds a run for their money, a Min Pin will seldom be in line when class awards are given for high scores in obedience. This is not because they're not intelligent enough to learn but because they're intelligent enough to learn that they would rather

This Min Pin is doing his time on the pause table before being instructed by his handler to continue with the rest of the agility course.

just have fun instead of following the rules. The people who train Min Pins for obedience do so for the pure joy of working with their dog and the challenges that doing so will invariably bring.

No matter what activities you want to eventually enjoy with your dog, obedience classes are a good place to begin. Certainly a dog who has been through at least basic obedience is easier to live with. And in fact, a dog who excels at obedience techniques is usually happier than others, because he masters exactly what he needs to do to please you as he learns what your basic commands really mean. If you decide that you won't be trying for obedience titles, you can be a little less structured with your training and focus more on the bonding aspect of the training. As I noted earlier, almost anything you do with your dog will be made easier if he has good basic manners and knows to obey your commands.

Entering the Competition

There are varying levels in obedience classes that range from the novice, Companion Dog (CD); through open, Companion Dog Excellent (CDX); to utility, Utility Dog (UD). For each level of class, a dog must earn (or "qualify" for) three "legs" to achieve a title.

Each leg will have the dog competing for at least 170 out of 200 possible points.

Each dog is judged on heeling on and off lead at varying speeds, sitting, staying with other dogs on command while the owner steps away from him, and also standing for a brief examination by the judge in the Companion Dog class.

The Companion Dog Excellent class will require your Min Pin to work completely off leash, perform all the exercises mentioned above for extended lengths of time, jump over obstacles, and retrieve.

The Utility Dog must complete the above requirements but obey visual commands instead of verbal ones. Your Min Pin will have more difficult obstacles and maneuvers, and he will have to perform scent tests.

Remember to have fun, and make sure that your Min Pin is enjoying himself as well. It's easy to get wrapped up in trying to achieve perfect scores and forgetting that you're both there to enjoy

Min Pins can do all sorts of things and are usually eager to try them, but it's up to you to keep them safe while they're doing them.

What (and What Not) to Wear: Tracking

Certainly, anyone who goes into a field in a rural area where hunters could possibly be lurking should wear at least one (if not several) bright orange or other fluorescent-colored pieces of outerwear. Footwear should be chosen depending on the type of terrain and what type of walking you may be required to do. Clothing should be loose, layered, and comfortable. No matter the weather, take along at least a light windbreaker to protect you against a sudden rain shower.

your comradeship. Your partnership should be obvious to everyone who sees you. Your Min Pin should obey you because he loves and respects you and wants to please you and not because he fears you or fears your displeasure if he fails. You should be a well-oiled machine, happy just to be working together.

AGILITY TRIALS

Since agility made its debut as simply an entertainment program at the 1979 Crufts Dog Show in England, it has been growing in popularity both in the dog community and with spectators by leaps and bounds. Agility is a great spectator sport, certain to get everyone on their feet as they watch with bated breath while dog and handler race around a timed course. Without a doubt, there could be no breed more suited to an agility course than the athletic and agile Min Pin.

It is anyone's guess as to who set up the first agility course, but they are loosely modeled after the courses used for equestrian jumpers competitions. Over the years, additional obstacles were added, the scoring systems were changed, and as is true with all sports, the definition of "perfection" changed with each stellar performance from an outstanding dog and handler.

Although the layout of the course may vary from trial to trial (set up according to the judge), some of the obstacles will always be used in one form or another. These include the A-frame, collapsed tunnel, dog walk, pause table, seesaw, weave poles, and the hoop jump. Various other jumps may also be added from time to time. Dogs are judged on their speed and agility in performing the obstacles.

Novice dogs compete on a simple course, working up to more complex courses that will truly test their skill and agility. This is one event in which the handler must be as fit as the dog, as they will be running around the course with their dog. Although they can't touch their canine partner, they are allowed to shout commands and encouragement and give the dog hand or voice signals. A dog may be the fastest on the field, but points are counted off for taking down any of the jump bars, failing to take a jump, going over or around the obstacles out of order, or failing to completely touch what is referred to as the "contact zone" on each obstacle or failing to finish within the judge's allotted time.

TRACKING

The ability of a dog to follow a scent that is hours or even days old over inhospitable terrain and in inclement weather is forever a mystery to humans. Most Min Pin owners who train their dogs to track believe that this is the ideal activity for any Min Pin. The dogs get to use the wonderful extrasensory perceptions with which nature and heredity have blessed them, and no other animals are harmed or killed in the process.

No matter how well a dog tracks, he cannot enter a competition before being certified by an AKC-approved tracking judge. To receive this certification, the dog must pass a test of complexity equivalent to the Tracking Dog (TD) test, and the test must take place under the conditions to be expected at an AKC-approved event. This is not a simple matter of taking your dog into a field and asking him to follow a scent. The tracking course is a complex network, carefully laid by skilled tracklayers. They must follow the exact directives of the AKC guide.

What elusive item will your Min Pin be tracking? For the TD test, a wallet or glove is the usual article of choice. The article is placed on the track before the dog or handler is allowed to see any part of the track.

After a dog has achieved his TD title, he can begin working on a TDX. The TDX course is longer and offers more obstacles and changes of terrain. It also allows for the crossing of tracks and for four personal items to be dropped along the track.

The AKC also offers a Variable Surface Tracking Test (VST), which is an even more competitive tracking event, for dogs who have earned their TD or TDX titles.

Chapter 8

HEALTH

of Your Miniature Pinscher

The right diet, sufficient exercise, and good grooming will go far in keeping your Min Pin in good health. In addition to these day-to-day aspects of your dog's care, you'll need to be aware of certain conditions that can develop and how to address them. You'll also want to have a strong relationship with your Min Pin's veterinarian, because you'll be trusting this individual to provide your dog with good professional care and you with good professional guidance. Here's what you'll need to know to be sure that your Min Pin lives the longest, healthiest life possible.

CHOOSING A VETERINARIAN

After you've found the breeder you want to work with, making the choice of who you will trust with the health care of your best friend is one of the most important decisions you will make. Make certain you select a vet you can trust, one who will truly listen to you, and someone you can consider a friend. Also, although proximity of the office shouldn't be a factor for routine medical care, it can be the difference between life or death for your pet in the case of an emergency. If the veterinarian you choose as your general practitioner is quite a distance from your home, it would be a good idea to have a "backup vet" or emergency pet hospital that is closer to your home.

You should ask your friends, family, and coworkers who they visit and why. People who really love their pets will be able to direct you to a vet who truly cares about animals and their welfare and who doesn't see her clinic only as a business. When you've narrowed down your choices, make an appointment to talk to each veterinarian (and her office staff) in person. Ask questions, and be wary of any clinic that doesn't have someone willing to take the time to answer your questions and make you feel comfortable. If they don't find time for you, they may not be willing to spend enough time on your dog when he needs them. Ask about their regular and emergency hours. Also ask about tattooing or microchip services. Inquire about their boarding facilities and if they have financing available in case of an emergency that is beyond your ability to pay immediately. Check out alternative practices they provide or recommend, such as acupuncture, acupressure, holistic, or homeopathic medicine. Ask whether they offer them directly, and if not, whether they approve of them. Would they be willing to direct you to a clinic that could provide those services if they became necessary?

Just because you start using one veterinarian doesn't mean you should stay with her if you are uncomfortable with her or her facility or with any aspect of your pet's care. If you don't feel that your new vet is truly listening to you or considering your observations and opinions regarding your pet, it's time to try someone different. The vet you and your Min Pin deserve is someone who is always willing to listen to your suggestions and observations about your dog.

A Puppy's First Vet Trip

Most breeders will ask that you have your new Min Pin thoroughly examined by a veterinarian within a certain length of time after purchase to agree with her own vet's assessment that the puppy is healthy and ready to begin a wonderful new life with you.

Although your breeder should have told you about any major health problems your dog may have, your vet may uncover something that she and her vet may have missed. Don't panic. Some problems your vet might find during this initial checkup are actually quite common and shouldn't require more than a quick call to the breeder to tell her of the findings. For example, there is a well-known saying among dog people—nothing is definite except death, taxes, and dogs have worms. No matter how well the breeder may have maintained your Min Pin's surroundings or how often a vet has checked the puppy during the first weeks of his life, internal parasites (especially roundworms) may show up on the fecal examination the veterinarian will do during your visit. All that's usually required is a single dose of dewormer (most vets use a paste formula that puppies actually find quite tasty) and a return checkup in a few weeks to make sure the worms are all gone and the puppy hasn't picked up new ones. Other internal parasites that plague dogs include whipworms, tapeworms, hookworms, and other pests such as coccidiosis and giardiasis. While it is true that most of these are easily treated (I'll discuss parasites in greater detail later in this chapter), it's very important to take care of the situation as quickly as possible. You should tell the breeder that your vet found parasites in your puppy so that she can treat the ones she has left with her.

Your vet might also find a small umbilical hernia. This, too, is nothing to panic about, although the breeder should have already mentioned it to you, if she was aware of it. Umbilical hernias are actually quite common, especially in puppies born to first-time mothers who either bite the umbilical cord too close to the stomach or damage the cord through excessive licking. Most umbilical hernias are caused by a delayed closure of the umbilical ring. These

Tips for Choosing the Right Vet for Your Dog

It's a good idea to always check with the Veterinary Medical Board to see if any complaints have been filed in connection with the veterinarian you are considering.

Make sure that your new vet likes dogs. Surprisingly enough, some veterinarians don't care for dogs or are even allergic to them. You might ask in conversation whether she herself has a dog. This can open up the avenue to find out if she is truly a dog person. Ask if she has other Min Pin clients and whether she is familiar with the genetic and usual health issues of a Min Pin.

Ask if she is willing to consider your opinions in all aspects of your pet's care.

Find out whether she or her clinic staff are available for after-hours emergency care. If they do not provide emergency service, get them to refer you to a clinic that does as a "backup" veterinarian.

Watch the interaction between vet and vet technicians. Are they friendly? Do courtesy and politeness rule the day?

Check if somebody will be with your pet through the night in case of an illness or accident that requires an overnight stay.

Ask if the office accepts insurance plans (if you have one) or credit cards or payment plans if you don't.

Trust your nose as well as your instincts when choosing a clinic. Although it's inevitable that a vet clinic will have animal and medical odors, there should be no overwhelming smells that suggest animals are not kept clean while in the care of the clinic's staff.

Lastly, but perhaps most importantly, rely on your gut instinct. If you feel uncomfortable, keep looking.

Making the Vet's Office a Happy Place

With proper training, visiting the vet can be a positive experience for your Min Pin rather than a scary expedition. While your pet is healthy, take him to the vet's office and feed him some treats, and then take him home. A few days later, take your Min Pin back and have some of the clinic staff give him cookies. Then, take him home. The next time, have him do some basic obedience routines in the office, and praise him, give him a treat or two, and take him home. By this time, he should realize that the vet's clinic is a good place to be. If you always have treats with you at the clinic, he'll be so excited about getting unlimited treats that the unpleasantness of an exam (and perhaps vaccinations or treatment) will not seem quite so terrible. (Be sure to get your vet's permission before you give treats to your dog in the office. There are some times, such as before surgery, that your dog shouldn't eat anything.)

Not only should you make your vet trips pleasant for your Min Pin, but you should make them as easy as possible on the clinic staff. For example, if your Min Pin is prone to submissive urination when picked up by strangers, warn whoever might be holding him during an exam. (Note that at some veterinary clinics, the vet permits owners to participate in the entire office visit. If you can, find a vet who will allow you to stay with your dog throughout the examination process.) If your Min Pin is prone to nipping or snapping, either muzzle him before you get to the clinic, or warn the staff in plenty of time so that they can muzzle him before he gets too upset. Long before you visit the vet clinic, get your Min Pin used to having all parts of his body touched, particularly problem areas that may require routine checkups.

will almost always get smaller and will likely disappear within six months. If it doesn't disappear on its own, the surgery to repair it is relatively simple and can be done quite easily when the dog is neutered.

Should your vet find an inguinal hernia (a bulge appearing in the groin), you should immediately call the breeder to discuss some sort of reimbursement or replacement. The surgery to repair such a hernia is a necessity, and it can be quite complex and expensive.

If you've chosen a male Min Pin, the vet should check to make sure that both testicles have descended into the sac. If they haven't, neutering the dog will be more costly and more invasive. The breeder should have made this clear to you before purchase, and in fact, it should have been covered in your contract.

Once you're sure your young Min Pin is healthy, you can all relax and begin to enjoy each other's company. Your vet will likely set you up with a schedule for checkups and vaccinations as well as for other preventive medicine.

PHYSICAL EXAMS

Just as humans should see a doctor on a regular basis, so should your Min Pin have regular physical examinations. Although the techniques may differ between canine and human doctors, the reason for regular checkups is the same. Preventive medicine is preferable to having to treat an illness or disease. And the earlier a malady is detected, the better the chances of a successful treatment and a full recovery for your Min Pin.

An annual examination will help the doctor assess the health of your Min Pin and recommend care. Although you would likely become aware of most problems yourself (often discovered while grooming or stroking your dog), some problems are not noticeable to anyone other than a trained medical expert. Annual physicals usually include checking the dog's temperature, pulse, respiration, weight, eyes, ears, mouth and throat, coat and skin, lymph nodes, abdomen, bones and joints, heart and lungs, and the perineum and reproductive organs. Your vet will also take a fecal sample to look for internal parasites.

It's possible that your Min Pin may need a thorough dental cleaning at some point. Your veterinarian should check your pet's teeth during all well-pet visits and tell you when it's necessary. This procedure requires anesthesia in most cases, so it's a good idea to schedule cleanings along with any other surgical needs that arise, such as neutering, or when your pet is being x-rayed for his OFA (Orthopedic Foundation for Animals) screening. If your pet has bad breath that can't be explained by something he ate, chances are very good that he either has tonsillitis or his teeth need a good, deep cleaning.

A physical examination should include a manual going-over of your dog's entire body.

You should ask your vet to trim your dog's nails while you are at the clinic unless you're taking your dog to a professional groomer (or perhaps trimming his toenails yourself when you groom him). Most vets will do this for a nominal fee. Long toenails are not only a hazard to your clothing and skin, but they can be easily snagged and torn, which can cause pain and discomfort to your pet. Long nails also place undue stress on the joints of the paws that can in turn cause long-term problems.

VACCINATIONS

For many years, it went without question that puppies began a vaccination routine at six weeks of age, receiving booster vaccinations for the next six weeks. Dogs were invariably given annual vaccinations on an annual basis throughout their lifetime. Today, many veterinarians are questioning this inoculation regime. Some assert that vaccines do far more harm than good and that the risks of vaccination without first checking a dog's immunity levels far outweigh the possible benefits.

You should discuss a vaccination schedule with your veterinarian after doing as much research as possible on the subject. Together, you can decide what the best schedule is for your Min Pin. Your veterinarian may provide routine vaccinations against canine distemper, infectious canine hepatitis or adenovirus, leptospirosis, parvovirus, coronavirus, parainfluenza, bordetella, Lyme disease, and rabies. The following brief synopsis will give you an idea of what these diseases entail.

Distemper is a highly contagious, often fatal virus that affects a dog's respiratory, gastrointestinal, and nervous systems. Generally, this virus spreads as an airborne infection, so vaccination is the only effective control. *Adenovirus* (also known as infectious

Vaccinations are necessary to protect against potentially fatal diseases.

hepatitis) is a viral disease that affects the liver and cells lining the blood vessels, causing high fever, thirst, loss of appetite, abdominal pain, liver damage, and hemorrhage. *Parvovirus* is an unfortunately very common and deadly viral infection; the symptoms of this disease include diarrhea, fever, and vomiting. Parvovirus is usually seen in younger dogs, and it can kill puppies very quickly, especially tiny breeds such as Min Pins. *Coronavirus* is a highly contagious viral infection of the gastrointestinal tract, with symptoms that are almost identical to those of parvo, but not as deadly. *Leptospirosis* is an extremely contagious disease (oftentimes carried by rats and mice) that spreads through contact with the nasal secretions, urine, or saliva of infected animals and can affect humans as well. The ailment causes inflamed kidneys, fever, vomiting, and diarrhea. Liver damage can also occur in severe cases. *Parainfluenza* virus is one of a number of infectious agents that cause what is often called "kennel cough." The disease is highly contagious and attacks the respiratory system, resulting in a dry, hacking cough. *Rabies* is an always fatal infection of the central nervous system that affects all mammals. It is most often seen in raccoons, bats, skunks, foxes, domestic dogs and cats, and humans. Because rabies poses a serious public health threat, it is imperative that your puppy be vaccinated against this disease, and most states require it.

Young puppies can quickly pick up and spread diseases.

Remember, most vaccines must be given over a period of time and require multiple veterinary visits, including annual booster shots. So check with your veterinarian and follow her suggestions for a vaccination schedule for your Min Pin. You should be aware that there is no such thing as a risk-free medical treatment or preventive. Any drug or vaccine carries some risk with its use, and there will be some patients who will suffer from its administration. When considering what schedule you wish to follow with your Min Pin's vaccinations, you should carefully balance the risks associated with the treatment/preventive against your dog's risk of catching, as well as surviving, the disease at hand.

SPAYING AND NEUTERING

You should spay your female or neuter your male Min Pin as soon as he or she has reached the age of six months. Although some veterinarians now advocate performing sterilization surgeries even younger, most agree that around six months is a good age for the surgery.

The Importance of Altering Your Dog

Perhaps you've considered breeding your Min Pin. If you purchased the dog on a Limited Registration from the breeder, however, you should have been advised that his offspring would not be eligible for registration. Other than that reason, there are dozens of others why your pet Min Pin should be spayed or neutered. If you want to produce genetically and physically healthy and happy puppies, it is very expensive and time consuming. Good dog breeding requires a tremendous amount of effort. By the time you've picked out a good female representative of the breed, waited for her to grow up both physically and emotionally (a minimum of two years), picked out the best dog to mate her with (one who may be clear across the country), gone through all the necessary genetic health checks she needs, and made certain that the prospective sire has passed the same health checks, you've already invested a massive amount of time, money, and effort. Then you still have to pay a stud fee or permit the stud owner to select her choice puppy from your litter (which will in turn give you less money from puppy sales). You will have extra expenses during your dog's pregnancy for higher quality food, prenatal checks by your veterinarian, as well as the time and expense of actually whelping the litter. These expenses can skyrocket if your bitch requires a C-section (not unusual) or dies (also, sadly, not uncommon) and you have to add the expense of missed work for vet trips, extra care, and perhaps even hand-raising the litter.

If you do breed a litter of Min Pins, you will need to keep the puppies for a minimum of eight weeks before choosing responsible homes for them. (It's illegal to sell puppies younger than eight weeks of age in many states.) And it's amazing how much puppy kibble baby Min Pins can eat and how quickly it can be turned into massive piles of puppy poop during the weeks after the mother stops taking care of her offspring. Then, you'll have the expense and hassle of advertising for good homes for your puppies, as well as screening prospective buyers. It doesn't end with the sale of the puppy, either. Responsible breeders follow through with checkups for several months at least to make sure that all is going well with the puppy in his new home.

Your litter of Min Pin puppies will require veterinary visits at three to five days and again at three weeks and six weeks for fecal examinations to check for internal parasites and to begin their vaccination schedule. (Remember, you have to multiply all these expenses by the number of puppies in your litter, which can quickly total up to an astronomical vet bill.)

If all the puppies survive and are placed in other homes, you run the risk of having dissatisfied customers later on, and because a conscientious breeder will offer to take puppies back who don't work out in their new homes, you could end up with more than you bargained for all around.

Breeders count themselves extremely lucky if they can financially break even on a litter, and most admit that it's more likely that a litter will put their bottom line in the red rather than in the black. Breeding a litter should never consist of simply breeding your bitch to the dog down the road just because he is of the opposite sex, is a registered dog of the same breed, and is nearby. The resulting puppies may not even resemble purebred Min Pins, and you run the risk of them having multiple genetic problems. Yes, you can cut corners and produce a litter with much less time and money invested, but all you will be doing will be adding to the pet overpopulation problem. If you don't have a good working knowledge of canine genetics to carefully plan your breeding, you can create dogs with

Breeding is best left to those who understand its many potential problems and who can properly raise and care for puppies.

Puppies who are physically and mentally sound are the result of very careful breeding.

health and temperament problems that you likely won't have the experience or knowledge to handle.

Many people choose to breed their Min Pin because they want a carbon copy of their dog, and that isn't going to happen. No matter how special your Min Pin is, his puppies are not guaranteed to look or act at all like their parent. After all, half of the puppy's genes will be from another dog. The best bet in finding a dog "just like yours" is to go back to the same breeder and get a closely related puppy.

Many old wives' tales survive regarding breeding dogs. One is that every bitch should have a litter, even if she is to be spayed afterward. There is no logical foundation for this idea. Bitches aren't "improved" by having puppies. Instead, they undergo hormonal temperament changes, which are hard on them physically and can shorten their life. Also an unspayed Min Pin will have a far greater risk of mammary cancer than one who has been spayed.

Perhaps you believe that simply because your dog is registered, he or she should be bred. Actually, a registered dog, no matter which kennel club he or she is registered with, has no inherent merit other than being (supposedly) a purebred. Most registries don't make any assertions of quality in the dogs listed in their registry. They do not restrict the breeding of those dogs; therefore, there is no guarantee that a "registered dog" is necessarily a good representative of his or her breed.

Unless your Min Pin was purchased as a show dog, has completed his show career, and has also been deemed worthy of being bred by his breeder, do the responsible thing, and have your dog spayed or neutered. And love your Min Pin for what he is, not for what he could produce.

PARASITES

Vigilant parasite control, both external and internal, is important for both the comfort and health of your Min Pin. He should get a fecal exam performed every time he visits the veterinarian, and appropriate parasite control measures should be taken, especially if your dog has to be treated for flea or worm infestations routinely. Your veterinarian can tell you what parasites tend to be more common where you live, what treatments work best in your specific area, and what preventive measures you should take for the specific parasites your pet seems to pick up most frequently.

A Good Offense

Just as in people, the best healthcare is preventive. I encourage the following measures to keep your dog in your home, instead of at the vet's office:

- Buy your Min Pin from a reputable breeder who will stand behind the health of the dogs she produces. It's a proven fact that puppy mill Min Pins are more susceptible to health problems and genetic defects because their parents most likely did not receive adequate prenatal care or genetic testing. And the choice to breed was made with only money in mind—not bettering the breed.

- Don't overfeed your Min Pin. Obesity is harmful to your Min Pin's heart, spine, and joints, and it makes him more susceptible to other health issues.

- Keep a good grooming routine. Religiously clean your Min Pin's ears once a week, trim the toenails once every two weeks, and check for full or impacted anal glands.

- Give your Min Pin regular monthly heartworm medication, and check for fleas and ticks on a daily basis.

- Immunize your dog for distemper, parvovirus, hepatitis, leptospirosis, and parainfluenza.

- Do not let your Min Pin climb long flights of stairs or jump off objects such as beds, couches, or porches. Be especially careful to prevent this type of activity when your dog is under one year of age.

- Never let your Min Pin wander loose in the neighborhood. A Min Pin is safest in a secure, fenced area or on a leash. Never allow him outdoors unsupervised and unprotected.

- If there is any sign of a medical problem, contact your veterinarian immediately. Don't wait until a problem becomes an emergency situation to seek help.

Internal Parasites

It is true that all dogs will, at some time during their life, have worms, no matter how vigilant their owner is about parasite control, so don't panic if your dog gets fecal exam results that indicate he has worms.

Many types of internal parasites and worms exist. They include:

- **Giardia** *(Giardia lamblia):* Probably the most common of the canine parasites—it's estimated that half of the puppies in the United States are affected.

- **Roundworm** *(Toxocara canis):* Roundworms are extremely common. Nearly all puppies are born with roundworms, which they acquire from their mother. Older dogs are less likely to be affected, but they can pick them up from infected soil (which is the main reason why you should always pick up your pet's feces immediately—and why you should keep

Playing outdoors is one of a dog's greatest pleasures. What they pick up while outside can be harmful, though, so be aware of what your dog may be exposed to while outdoors.

your Min Pin away from other dogs' feces.)

- **Hookworm *(Ancylostoma caninum):*** Hookworms not only plague dogs, but these worms can also be passed to humans. Dogs with hookworm infestation may have blood in their stool, will be likely to lose weight, and will show gastric distress.

- **Whipworm *(Trichuris vulpis):*** Whipworms are the most challenging of all worms to destroy, both in your dog's system and in infested soil. Severe infestations of whipworm can give a dog colitis and can prove fatal.

- **Tapeworm *(Dipylidium caninum):*** Tapeworms are visible in your Min Pin's stool, and you may see what looks like tiny grains of rice around your dog's anus. These are actually dried tapeworm segments. If your dog has fleas, it's likely that he has tapeworms, too. Regular dewormers are not effective against tapeworms, and your pet will require special treatment.

- **Heartworm *(Dirofilaria immitis):*** Your Min Pin should have a good heartworm preventive throughout his lifetime. As the name suggests, these worms travel through your dog's bloodstream to his heart, where they attach to the lining, doing great damage to the heart muscle, as well as blocking arteries. The preventive is a simple procedure, while the treatment for heartworm can be severe and costly. An added benefit of keeping your Min Pin on heartworm preventive is that it will also help prevent him from contracting other types of internal parasites.

See your veterinarian about treatment and prevention options for these internal parasites.

External Parasites

Your Min Pin will also likely pick up fleas and ticks on his forays into the great outdoors. While fleas are simply pesky to most dogs (except for those with sensitive skin or severe allergies), ticks can create a serious health hazard for you and your pet if you live in areas where Lyme disease is found. Your veterinarian can tell you whether Lyme disease is a problem in your area and can vaccinate your dog against the disease if necessary.

Flea and tick control can be applied topically or given orally on a once-a-month schedule that is usually sufficient for most pets. However, to keep your Min Pin flea-free, you may need to treat your pet's surroundings if you live in some areas, especially if you live in a hot, humid climate. There are wonderful species specific insect growth regulators on the market that do no harm to the environment and work by making insects sterile upon contact. Although you may have to spray with a chemical insecticide occasionally, remember that these harsh sprays are not species specific, and you could end up creating even more of a problem if you kill "good" bugs along with the "bad." If you do use chemicals for flea prevention, be sure to keep them away from your Min Pin, and don't let him in the yard until the spray has completely dried and into the house until it is well aired out. (You might do well to follow those same instructions yourself!)

There are products you can apply to your Min Pin's skin that will help ward off fleas.

Caring for Anal Glands

Although it's probably the very least pleasant aspect of dog ownership, it's important that you check your Min Pin's anal glands regularly. If you see him scooting around on his rear end, he's not trying to be funny; instead, it's likely that an anal gland irritation or impaction exists that is either itching him or causing him pain. If left untreated, these glands can quickly become infected, which is not only very painful for the dog, but it requires treatment that you both will likely find quite unpleasant.

The anal glands can be easily found at about the eight o'clock and four o'clock positions on each side of your Min Pin's anus. The fluid contained in these sacs is extremely foul smelling. Many dog behaviorists and researchers agree that it is this odor that provides the means of identification between individual animals (which explains why dogs go around sniffing each other there). Normally these sacs empty with every bowel movement, and sometimes a pet will express his glands when he's scared, nervous, or upset. However, factors such as obesity, internal parasites, allergies, and low-fiber diets can lead to anal gland impaction.

Emptying the sacs is quite simple (although admittedly quite unpleasant for everyone involved). Simply place your thumb and index finger just below the anus, covering the anal opening with a tissue to catch the fluid, and squeezing gently, press inward and upward on the sacs simultaneously. This should cause the fluid within to be evacuated. Be prepared for a very oily, foul-smelling elimination that is not water-soluble and therefore is very hard to remove from clothes or skin. If you should have an accident, use isopropyl alcohol followed by soap and water to remove the odor.

If you decide not to do this yourself, your vet or a local groomer will do it for you for a nominal fee.

PROBLEMS SEEN IN THE MINIATURE PINSCHER

Min Pins are a fairly hardy breed, but there is no breed that has absolutely no genetic health issues. Fortunately, the list of possible genetic health problems in the Min Pin isn't nearly as long as that of some other breeds. The following are the most probable health issues a vet is likely to see in the Miniature Pinscher:

Leg Injuries

Although leg injuries are not a genetic issue, they're very common in Min Pins and are the leading reason that Min Pins end up in a vet's office. Because these are small dogs, it is especially important to monitor their activities, and in particular, to watch children around them. The Min Pin loves to run and play with kids, and he has no idea that he isn't as big as they are. If a child falls on or trips over a Min Pin, a broken leg is not an unlikely result. Moreover, most Min Pins apparently have no idea that they can't fly, since most will bounce off of furniture that is far above their head. Sometimes the landing isn't as foolproof as they expected, and their fragile bones can't take the stress.

Patellar Luxation

Patellar luxation ("patellar" meaning "knee," "luxation" meaning "dislocation") is a condition that affects many small breeds, including the Min Pin. Also known as "slipped stifles," it can cause either a minimum of pain and discomfort and only occasional limping, or it can become more severe if the condition is not corrected or treated, to the point that the dog is in constant pain and can become unable to use one, or even in rare cases, both rear legs. Mild cases are usually treated with total rest, while more severe cases must be corrected surgically. Because this is believed to be a genetic condition, dogs with slipped stifles should not be bred.

Legg-Calve-Perthes Disease

Legg-Calve-Perthes disease (LPCD) is a hereditary disorder of the hip joint. Min Pins are considered to be at risk for the disease, and it is usually diagnosed between the ages of four months and one year of age. Caused when the blood supply to the head of the femur is stopped, it eventually results in the total degeneration of the joint. Although different treatments may be offered depending on the severity of the problem (and in some cases the damaged

The Miniature Pinscher is a fairly hardy breed, although certainly not immune to potential health problems.

You'll want to check your Min Pin's eyes frequently as he ages to determine if he's affected by progressive retinal atrophy.

areas will heal to a certain degree), eventually, the only recourse is surgery to remove the head of the femur. Because of the hereditary nature of this issue, all breeding stock should be tested and cleared of the disorder with the Orthopedic Foundation for Animals.

Progressive Retinal Atrophy (PRA)

The retina is the "transmitter" of the eye, designed to receive light from outside the eye and transmit it to the brain, where the brain transfers the signal into vision. When deterioration (atrophy) of the retinal cells occurs, depending on the type of PRA, it brings varied stages of blindness.

COMMON CANINE HEALTH PROBLEMS

Some health concerns arise in all breeds of dog. Because your dog can't tell you that something is bothering him, you'll need to keep an eye out for signs of illness.

Allergies

Poor skin quality can be a sign of an allergic reaction, and your Min Pin can have a reaction to almost anything he comes in contact with, from the cleaner you use on your floor or carpet to the detergent you use on his bedding. If your pet has skin allergies or sensitive skin, it will only take one fleabite to start an allergic reaction. Be aware that over 20 percent of dog allergies are a reaction to something in their food. Before you spend a lot of money on allergy testing and inoculations, try switching your pet's food to something with a different base ingredient. For example, if your dog food has a chicken base, try feeding one that is made from lamb and rice or beef. With pet supermarket shelves full of good-quality kibble, you should be able to find something that will suit your Min Pin's needs and nip his allergies in the bud.

Bloat

If your Min Pin is showing signs of digestive stress but can belch, pass a stool normally, or vomit, chances are that he's just experiencing an upset stomach (unless you think it's likely that he's eaten something harmful). If he can't vomit, belch, or pass a stool, if he whines when you push on his stomach, or if he's salivating excessively and showing evidence of abdominal pain, time is definitely of the essence, and he should see an emergency vet immediately—these may be signs of bloat.

If your dog is suffering from bloat, the first thing a vet will do is to put a large needle directly into your dog's stomach (through the outside abdominal wall) or put a long plastic tube down his throat into his stomach. The relief for your dog is almost immediate, once the air that's trapped inside has a way to get out. Your dog will be given medicines and started on an IV until he is stable enough for surgery. The purpose of surgery is to see how much damage has been done internally, and your vet may also decide to tack the stomach to the abdominal wall so that bloat doesn't occur again.

It's always better to be prepared and never need to put the knowledge to use than to be unprepared in an emergency and risk your pet's life. To avoid risks of bloat, feed two small meals a day instead of one large one, and never allow your dog to exercise or work on a full stomach, especially if he's elderly or recuperating from an illness.

Older dogs who engage in strenuous physical exercise, especially after eating, may experience bloat, which is a true medical emergency.

Healthy Holidays

The holidays bring about an entirely new set of worries when it comes to keeping your Min Pin healthy. Things that are safe and fun for humans can actually be quite toxic—and even potentially deadly—to your Min Pin.

Holiday Parties

A holiday party can be a threat to your Min Pin unless everyone who attends is dog savvy and knows the rules about what is acceptable for dogs to eat and drink. Some people think it's funny to give a dog alcoholic beverages. They wouldn't think your drunken Min Pin was so funny if they had to sit up with him all night or pay the vet bill to keep him alive after he suffered gastrointestinal irritation, tremors, difficulty breathing, or a coma from alcohol poisoning. If he doesn't suffer serious (even fatal) damage from the alcohol, he may still be a very sick dog for a while. Think about the difference in size between a human and your little Min Pin, and do the math to see how little alcohol it would take to do a lot of damage.

Party foods can be a danger to your Min Pin as well. Candies and gum that contain the sweetener xylitol can cause problems in dogs—including a fairly sudden drop in blood sugar, resulting in depression and seizures—especially if large amounts are eaten. Chocolate, in all forms—baking, semi-sweet, milk, and dark—can be potentially poisonous to your Min Pin, depending on the amount eaten and the type of chocolate. Vomiting, diarrhea, seizures, hyperactivity, and increased thirst, urination, and heart rate can be seen with the ingestion of as little as $1/4$ ounce (7.1 g) of baking chocolate by a 10-pound (4.5 kg) dog. Spicy and highly seasoned foods can cause stomach upset in most dogs and pancreatitis in Min Pins who are prone to the problem.

Even ordinary foods can harm your Min Pin if fed to him by unsuspecting guests. With "bloomin' onions" becoming popular party fare, it's important to know that onions can be extremely toxic to your Min Pin's system. They cause oxidative damage to the hemoglobin, which can result in acute anemia if your dog consumes enough of them. Either fresh or cooked onions can be toxic, and if enough are ingested, a dog might need a blood transfusion. In addition, hemoglobin can be passed in the urine, and if your dog is not kept well hydrated, the kidneys can be damaged as well. If you realize that your Min Pin has ingested onions, contact your veterinarian immediately and request emergency care.

Not only will your Min Pin possibly be at risk from foods or drink that your guests might share with him, but it's likely that he could suffer a great deal of stress if he hasn't been properly socialized around large groups of noisy people. Also, a careless guest is likely to leave a door open long enough for your Min Pin to escape without you knowing he's even missing in all the hubbub of the party.

It's best for him and for you that your dog be kept away from the festivities. Give him an acceptable treat, and perhaps allow him to come be part of the party on a supervised basis.

Electric Shocks

Most people who are very careful about their use of extension cords during the rest of the year can become lax on safety issues in the holiday rush. If you must run cords to holiday lighting, run them through a length of PVC piping so that they're not accessible to your Min Pin. Not only can your pet suffer electric shocks from holiday lights, but he can become entangled in strings of lights, which can cause burns and cuts.

Choking Hazards

Even the best housekeepers can't keep track of all the extra clutter that is amassed during the holiday season. From staples and rubber bands to glue and ornament hangers to small ornaments and packing peanuts, any small item is a potential choking hazard to a snoopy Min Pin.

Candles

The flame of a candle isn't the only hazard to your Min Pin. Dripping wax can be extremely painful and can cause deep skin burns. Candles should never be left burning in a room with an unsupervised Min Pin, not only for his personal safety but also because of the potential fire hazard to your entire home if they are knocked over.

Plants

Most plants purchased at holiday time can be toxic to animals. Holly, mistletoe, ivy, and poinsettias can cause problems ranging from a mild stomach upset to an extreme toxic reaction. The first symptoms include nausea, vomiting, diarrhea, and extreme drooling. You should seek medical attention immediately, as these indicators can be a precursor of a coma, central nervous system or cardiac problems, and even death. A Min Pin is so tiny that it doesn't take much of any toxin to cause him serious problems.

Make sure that you know how to contact your vet during what may be a very erratic holiday schedule for her. If your regular veterinary office will be closed, be certain that you have information for a backup vet as well as an emergency clinic for after-hours care.

Skin Issues

The skin is an excellent barometer for the overall health of a dog. Dry, itchy, red skin with scaly hairless patches and flakes of dandruff can be indicative of many things, from basic dry skin that can be treated by putting a teaspoon (4.9 ml) of vegetable oil on your pet's food each day, to demodectic or sarcoptic mange that must be treated by your veterinarian. As noted earlier, skin problems are also frequently caused by allergies.

ALTERNATIVE HEALTH CARE

Even the American Veterinary Medical Association (AVMA) is now fully open to the possibility of the benefits of alternative medicine. Known by several terms, including "alternative," "complementary," and "integrative," this field of medicine has been given the name Complementary and Alternative Veterinary Medicine (CAVM). Under this term, a growing number of healing methods can be found, most used throughout the ages, that pet owners are finding useful in not only keeping their pets healthy but in treating injury and illness. If possible, try to find a veterinarian who either ascribes to these beliefs or is at least open to the

Your Min Pin's overall well-being can be enhanced by the proper use of alternative health options.

possibilities. In the best-case scenario, you will find a veterinarian who believes that there should be a good mixture of the different practices, someone who will put both modern medicine and ancient tried-and-true methods to work to make your Min Pin's life longer, happier, and healthier. These ancient methods include (but are not limited to):

Acupuncture

Acupuncture is the Chinese practice of inserting needles into specific points (acupoints) along the "meridians" of the body. It is used to relieve pain, to induce surgical anesthesia, and for preventive as well as therapeutic purposes. The insertion of the needles stimulates the acupuncture points and alters the flow of chi (the vital force or energy of the body) throughout the body.

Aromatherapy

Aromatherapy is the use of essential plant oils to promote relaxation and to help relieve the symptoms of specific ailments. Essential oils are extremely concentrated and very fragrant extracts that are steamed from the blossoms, leaves, or roots of various plants. These oils can be applied through massage, as compresses on the skin, diffused into the air and inhaled, or mixed with water as a bath. Essential oils are so concentrated that they should be considered extremely toxic if they are ingested.

Ayurvedic Medicine

Ayurvedic medicine is a medical practice developed in India. In this form of healing, health is considered to be a delicate balance of the body's physical, emotional, and spiritual systems, while illness is proof of an imbalance. Illness can be detected by reading the pulse and the tongue. Treatments can include nutrition, massage, natural medications, meditation, and the like.

Chiropractic care can help keep a bouncy Min Pin on his toes.

Chiropractic

Chiropractic medicine is a system of healing based on the idea that the body has an innate, self-healing ability. Subluxations of the joints are believed to interfere with the body's ability to maintain good health. Through manipulations of the spine and other joints and muscles, the body is brought back into balance so that the neuromusculoskeletal system can again function smoothly.

Energy Medicine

This therapy uses an energy field (which can be electrical, magnetic, sonic, microwave, infrared, or acoustic) to detect and treat illness. A practitioner can identify imbalances in the energy fields of a patient's body, and using a chosen energy, can attempt to correct them.

Environmental Medicine

Environmental medicine is an approach that focuses on the role of allergens (both dietary and environmental) on a patient's health. Many chronic illnesses can be controlled or improved with the judicious use of environmental medicine.

Herbal Medicine

Herbal medicine involves the use of natural plants or substances derived from these plants to treat illness, prevent disease, and enhance the body's function. All parts of the plant may be used in herbal medicine, including the bark, leaves, stems, and roots, and can be prepared in many ways, including tonics, pills, powders, and extracts. There is no governing body to oversee the strengths of these herbal remedies (or how they are gathered, prepared, or prescribed). To avoid over- or under-dosages, herbal medicine should be used only under the guidance of a practitioner who is familiar with herbal medicine.

A Min Pin who radiates good health is one whose health is being tended to holistically, from an emotional as well as a physical perspective.

Holistic Medicine

As the name implies, holistic medicine views the patient as a "whole" body instead of just a particular disease or a list of symptoms. A holistic approach takes into consideration that a patient's mental, emotional, and spiritual state can affect his overall condition, and also that nutrition, environment, and lifestyle can positively or adversely affect a patient's body and can contribute to an illness. Holistic practitioners usually treat patients with a blend of traditional forms of treatment, such as medication and surgery, with alternative forms of treatment, such as acupuncture, chiropractic, or herbal medicine.

Homeopathy

A homeopathic approach to healing employs the philosophy of "like heals like." In this branch of medicine, treatments comprise substances that, in their undiluted state, can produce the symptoms of the disease in an otherwise healthy patient. The substances are diluted greatly in solutions that are then given to the patient. Homeopaths also usually believe that a patient's mental, physical, and emotional state must be addressed along with the body's medical symptoms and must be treated along with the symptoms for a full recovery to take place. Vaccines, which we are familiar with as a traditional medical procedure, might be considered a homeopathic medicine.

Massage is something you can do for your dog that will help both of you feel better.

Kinesiology

Kinesiologists use an investigation of the muscle-gland-organ link to find the cause of illnesses. Practitioners of applied kinesiology believe that muscles reflect the flow of a body's chi and that one can determine the health of body organs by measuring muscle resistance. Once the problem has been identified in this manner, a number of different treatment techniques may be employed to strengthen the involved muscles and restore good health to the patient.

Massage

Massage is a systematic therapeutic stroking or kneading of the body or part of the body. The manipulation of a body's soft tissue structure can reduce tension and stress, increase circulation, aid the healing of muscle and soft-tissue injury, control pain, and promote an overall sense of well-being.

N.A.E.T.

Nambrudripad's Allergy Elimination Technique (N.A.E.T.), is an approach to detecting and eliminating allergies. This combines kinesiology and Oriental medicine to clear symptoms of allergic reactions. The technique involves the stimulation of specific acupuncture points along the spinal column that are associated with individual organs of the body.

Excessive thirst can be a sign that something is physically upsetting your Min Pin.

Reflexology

Practitioners of reflexology believe that different regions of the feet correspond to particular body systems. The therapy involves manipulations of specific areas of the feet to eliminate energy blockages that produce disease in the associated organs.

Shiatsu

A shiatsu massage is a Japanese technique that uses finger and thumb pressure on precise body points to encourage a proper flow of chi throughout a patient's body. It is a form of acupressure.

TTouch

Tellington Touch ("TTouch") is a method of training and healing named for developer Linda Tellington-Jones. This technique uses a combination of specific touches, lifts, and movement exercises. The technique is believed to enable an animal to learn new behavior more easily, promote optimal health, and correct inappropriate behavior by eliminating many fear- and negative-reactive responses.

Therapeutic Touch

This is a method of healing that, despite its name, does not involve actual physical contact. The therapeutic touch practitioner aligns and balances the patient's natural energy field by moving her hands just above the patient's body. The healer attempts to focus positive energy to the patient to balance and unblock positive energy flows.

EMERGENCY PREPAREDNESS

While some emergency situations are readily apparent, others are less so. You should be familiar with your pet's baseline readings to evaluate how severe an emergency actually is and to have information to give your emergency vet when she is contacted. These baseline readings should include:

- *Your pet's rectal temperature:* Normal body temperature for a dog is 99°F (37.2°C) and 102.5°F (39°C). Learn how to take your Min Pin's temperature before you're in an emergency situation so that you will both be comfortable doing so. Using a well-lubricated thermometer properly shaken down to below 96°F (35.5°C), gently insert the bulb end of the thermometer into your Min Pin's rectum. Hold it firmly but gently in place for about one minute. It's a great help if someone will hold your dog's head to keep him standing in place.

• *Color of gums:* Some dogs routinely have paler or brighter gums than others, but they should never be bright rosy red or pale gray. Pale gums can indicate anemia or shock. Dark red ones can mean poisoning or a high fever. A yellow tinge is an indicator of liver dysfunction.

• *Heart rate:* The normal heart rate for a Min Pin is between 60 to 140 beats per minute. Check your dog occasionally when he is healthy to get a more accurate count of the rate that is typical for him. To check the heart rate, place your fingers on the femoral artery, which runs along the thigh bone on the inside of the rear leg about halfway between the hip and the knee. Using a stopwatch or clock with a third hand, count heartbeats for ten seconds and then multiply by six.

• *Respiration rate:* Most dogs breathe 10 to 30 times per minute. It's a good idea to ask your veterinarian what your Min Pin's average rate of respiration is so that you can tell if he is breathing erratically.

Gum color is one indication of good or poor health.

• *Capillary refill time (CRT):* The capillary refill time is the amount of time it takes for tissue to resume normal color after pressure has been applied and removed. To test CRT, firmly press your thumb on the gum near a canine tooth. Remove your thumb and note how long it takes for the white mark to return to pink. If it takes longer than two seconds, the situation may be critical. This is an indicator of circulatory

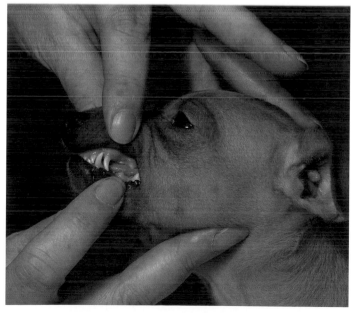

How To Perform the Heimlich Maneuver

Step-by-step instructions for doing the Heimlich Maneuver should be included in your first-aid kit.

Check for signs of choking: These include hard coughing, eyes bulging in panic because he can't breathe, and pawing at the mouth.

Clear the mouth: If the dog is conscious, pry open the mouth and look inside. Hold one hand over the top of the mouth, using your thumb and forefinger to press against the lips to get the mouth open. Pull the bottom jaw down with your other hand. Use your thumb and first finger to sweep the mouth and remove any foreign object.

Place dog on his side: If you can't see anything in your Min Pin's mouth, turn him on his side, with his head lower than his rear. Put something like a pillow under his rear end.

Find the bottom of the rib cage: Locate where the dog's ribs meet in the middle (sternum). Then go a few fingers-width below, toward the belly.

Press in and up: Put one hand at the spot you found and the other behind the dog's back for support. Use your hand on the bottom of the dog's rib cage, and press sharply in and up. Keep doing this until he expels what he was choking on. Try the next step if this one doesn't work.

Do artificial respiration, if necessary: If your dog is unconscious, keep him on his side, with his head lower than his rear. Extend the head gently up and out. Pull the tongue to the side. Do the compressions from the last step twice. Then, check the mouth for the object. Close the mouth, extend the head up, and give two breaths through the dog's nose until you see his chest rise. Repeat the compressions, the mouth check, and the two breaths until the dog is breathing again.

No matter what happens next, take your Min Pin to the vet immediately. If possible, have someone else drive to the vet while you are still working on your dog.

(heart) problems, shock, or dehydration.

- *Dehydration test:* To determine whether your Min Pin is dehydrated, pinch the skin and pull it up from the shoulders, and then release. Dehydrated skin holds the shape of the pinch; normal skin will retain its normal shape.
- *Responsiveness:* Normal dogs are alert, curious, and responsive. If your dog is slow to respond to being touched, does not respond to visual or auditory stimuli, seems sleepy or disoriented, is having seizures, or has no response to even pain stimulation (pinching between toes is a good stimulation when checking for response time), take your Min Pin to the vet immediately.

WHAT'S IN YOUR FIRST-AID KIT?

It's a great idea to keep a canine first-aid kit around the house for emergencies. You can use an old shoe box, a plastic container, or anything else that fits your needs. Make sure that the kit is clearly labeled, that everyone in the home knows where it is kept, and that it's located within easy reach.

Every well-stocked first-aid kit should have the following:

- Note card with phone numbers for your regular veterinarian, and emergency veterinarian, as well as local and national poison-control centers.
- Note card with baseline health information for your pet, including weight, temperature, blood panel results, and current vaccination records.
- Humane muzzle or old pantyhose for making a makeshift muzzle. (Even the most well-behaved dog will bite when he is in pain.)
- Material for bandaging, which should include sterile gauze pads of various sizes (differing widths) and of both stretchable and nonstretchable gauze; elastic bandages; plastic wrap for sealing wounds against dirt and air; bubble wrap (for splinting); and sterile tape.
- Blunt scissors (for trimming fur from wounds and cutting bandages/tape)
- 3 percent hydrogen peroxide (for cleansing wounds), or if necessary, to induce vomiting (give 1 to 3 teaspoons [4.9 to 14.8 ml] every ten minutes to induce vomiting)
- Tweezers or hemostats for removing foreign objects
- Lubricants (petroleum jelly, mineral oil)

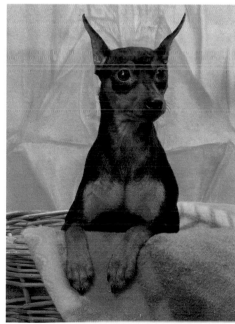

If your normally outgoing Min Pin seems lethargic or disoriented, suspect a physical problem.

- Styptic powder
- Antiseptic liquid soap
- Hot water bottle, heating pad, or hot/cold packs
- Cotton balls
- Sterile saline contact lens solution (for flushing wounds)
- Buffered aspirin (for pain)
- Antihistamine (for itching, stings, or bites, and as sedative if needed)
- Antidiarrheal medication
- Canine rectal thermometer

POISONOUS HOUSE AND GARDEN PLANTS

Always ask a garden expert if a plant is poisonous when ingested before you purchase new plants for the yard. While some plants are less toxic than others, all should be avoided when possible. The most common symptoms seen in pets who have ingested a toxic plant include swelling or irritation of the tongue, nausea, paralysis, salivation, and staggering. The list below shows what part of each plant is the most toxic.

Every first-aid kit should include a supply of gauze pads of varying sizes.

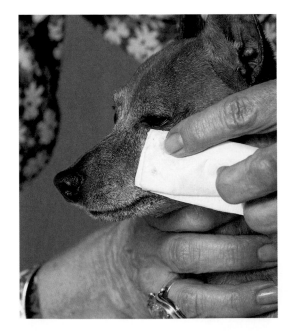

- Amaryllis (bulb)
- Apple (seeds can be fatal—cyanide poisoning occurs when eatenin large quantities)
- Apricot (pits)
- Autumn crocus (bulb)
- Azalea (all parts)
- Bleeding Heart (foliage, roots)
- Buttercups (all parts)
- Cactus (all parts)
- Caladium (leaves, roots—possibly fatal if large amounts ingested)
- Calla Lily (all parts, can be fatal)
- Castor Bean (seeds)
- Cherry Tree (leaves, twigs, seeds, tree bark, can be fatal due to cyanide poisoning if ingested)
- Chinaberry (all parts, can cause fatal convulsions)
- Crocus (all parts)
- Crown of Thorns (all parts)

Although they make for a lovely photo backdrop, some plants can be toxic to your Min Pin if he eats them.

- Daffodil (bulb, can be fatal)
- Delphinium (seeds and young plants)
- Dumb Cane (all parts)
- Elderberry (all parts, especially roots)
- Elephant's Ear (all parts)
- Four-o'clock (roots, seeds)
- Foxglove (leaves, seeds, can be fatal)
- Golden Chain (seeds, can be fatal)
- Holly (berries)
- Hyacinth (bulb, can be fatal)
- Hydrangea (all parts)
- Iris (underground stem, leaves)
- Ivy, Boston (all parts)
- Jonquil (bulb)
- Lantana (all parts, can be fatal)
- Larkspur (seeds, young plants, can be fatal)
- Lily of the Valley (leaves, flowers)
- Mistletoe (berries, can be fatal)
- Morning Glory (seeds)
- Mother-in-Law's Tongue (leaves)
- Narcissus (bulb)
- Oleander (leaves, branches)

A call to your veterinarian is essential if you suspect that your Min Pin has eaten something poisonous.

- Peach (pits, can be fatal due to cyanide poisoning)
- Peony (roots)
- Philodendron (all parts)
- Rhubarb (leaves and blades—leaf stalk is harmless)
- Skunk Cabbage (all parts)
- Tobacco (leaves)
- Wisteria (seeds, pods)
- Yew (seeds, foliage, bark, can be fatal)

If you believe that your Min Pin has ingested a toxic plant, get him to a veterinarian immediately. Wrap him in a blanket to avoid chilling from shock, and keep the dog as quiet as possible en route. Try to keep his head lower than his body to allow poisons to drain from the mouth. Also, take a portion of the suspected plant with you for positive identification. Do not administer first aid if your Min Pin is convulsing or unconscious.

If your veterinarian is unavailable, you can call the national Animal Poison Control Center for advice on what to do for your Min Pin. It is the only one of its kind in North America, and it acts as a 24-hour-a-day hotline center for animal poisoning inquiries from the United States, Mexico, and Canada. Have your credit card handy when you dial, as a nominal fee is charged to cover their expenses. The toll-free number is 1-800-548-2423.

LOST DOG!

Almost every dog owner will at some point experience the trauma of realizing that her dog isn't where he is supposed to be. What should you do if you couldn't find your dog? First of all, don't panic. Keep your wits about you, and think like a Min Pin. The chances of finding him are quite good if you act quickly and efficiently.

First, search your property thoroughly. Min Pins can get into some mighty strange places, and sometimes they will just sit patiently waiting to be rescued instead of making noises to alert you to their presence.

Walk the neighborhood, talk to everybody, and leave your cell phone number. Go to each house in the area where your Min Pin was lost, and talk to the residents. If possible, quickly make up a flyer with a small photo of your pet, a description, and your contact information. (It's not a good idea to post your home address on flyers for safety's sake, but be sure that a contact phone number is available, preferably a cell phone, that you can have with you at all times.) Leave one of these with each person you see, and if someone isn't home, leave it attached to the door.

Make a lot of noise while you walk around the neighborhood. Animals can hear you from great distances. Have all your family members call your Min Pin's name, and if your pet has a favorite squeaky toy, bring it along and use it to help you make familiar noises. Carry a box of your Min Pin's favorite biscuits, chews, or other treats, and rattle it loudly while calling his name. As important as it is to make lots of noise, it's equally important to remember to stop and be quiet occasionally in case your dog is making sounds to try to get your attention.

Bring a powerful flashlight (even during daylight hours). You'll want a strong flashlight with you for checking in dark spaces. A frightened Min Pin will likely hide in a dark place, and he may not come out to you if he is scared or so injured that he cannot move or make a sound. Check underneath cars and houses and inside storage sheds, garages, dumpsters, and behind outbuildings and woodpiles.

If your dog becomes lost, it's helpful to have a clear, full-body photo of him that you can distribute.

Place strong-scented articles outside your home to attract your pet. Animals find their way by scent as well as by sound. Place some of your dirty clothes, such as sweaty gym socks, t-shirts, and jogging suits, on the ground. Check back often to see if your Min Pin may be waiting patiently beside them. If the weather is cooperative, crate other family pets outside in a safe and secure area so that your lost Min Pin might smell them and return. Other pets may also make noise that would attract their lost comrade.

Call local veterinary offices. Check in with the veterinary clinics in your area to see whether your Min Pin was injured and taken to any of these offices

Keep your Min Pin safe by ensuring that the area you're in is completely fenced or that you always have a collar and leash on your dog.

or clinics for treatment.

Contact and visit your local animal control, humane societies, and animal shelters. In addition to the facilities in your immediate area, get in touch with those in surrounding areas, too. Leave flyers with a description of your Min Pin and your contact information. Check back with the staff daily, because they usually operate on a volunteer basis, and different people may be manning the office each day.

Post as many flyers as possible. Place flyers about your lost pet everywhere within a 1-mile (1.6-km) radius of where he was lost. Put ads in local newspapers, and ask your local radio station if it could mention your situation on the air.

Sadly, be aware that there are people in our society who prey upon victims by using "found" pets as a ploy. Oftentimes, they will have stolen the pet in the first place to have a reason to contact you. For that reason, you should never respond alone to a "found pet" contact. Take a friend with you, and meet in a public place. Also, never arrange to meet the person at your home unless she is a neighbor whom you know well.

When you have found your Min Pin, remember to go back and take down all the flyers you have posted, perhaps replacing a few with a new flyer expressing words of thanks to those who cared enough to send good thoughts or help with the recovery.

Keeping Your Min Pin Secure

Just as with veterinary medicine, prevention is the best option for keeping your Min Pin from getting lost in the first place. Always keep him confined to a fenced area when he is outdoors, unless he is on a leash or supervised in some other manner. Check fence perimeters and gates often to find potential escape routes. Also, always transport your Min Pin in a pet carrier to prevent him from escaping in case of an accident or a car door left open and unguarded a second too long.

Have good, clear photos of your Min Pin scanned and on your computer ready to use as quick identification. Have your Min Pin microchipped or tattooed so that a rescuer will have a way of contacting you to return him to his home. Always keep your Min Pin's rabies tag on his collar, not only as a means of identification but as proof that he has been inoculated in case he is accused of biting someone. In areas that are in a rabies alert stage, a tagless dog could be picked up and euthanized by authorities before you get a chance to retrieve him.

Train your Min Pin to come to one specific sound, no matter what. A whistle, a specific phrase, or a dog whistle will work fine. Use that phrase or sound before every meal so that the dog always associates it with something positive and is more likely to come to it when he finds himself outdoors and on his own.

Neuter your Min Pin to alleviate the wanderlust that many animals feel when their hormones start raging.

By taking the proper precautions from the beginning and having a good plan of action in case the worst-case scenario comes to be, your Min Pin will have an excellent chance of spending all his nights where he belongs—at home in the arms of his family.

THE AGING MIN PIN

There is no friend like an old friend. And no one could be dearer than an older Min Pin who has been beside you through good times and bad. Like an old married couple, you are aware of each other's likes and dislikes, and he instinctively seems to know when you need an exuberant dog kiss after a tough day at work. You have learned to depend on each other for comfort, for laughs, and for companionship when the rest of the world seems to have turned its back. As much as you need your Min Pin, he needs you now more than ever before; taking care of his special needs to ensure a long, healthy life proves your love for him will endure well into his golden years and beyond.

In general, senior Min Pins can't handle stress as well as they did when they were younger. Sudden changes in

As your Min Pin ages, he will need extra care and consideration.

routine, diet, or even the environment can play havoc with your older Min Pin's health. A dog's body changes as he grows older, just as our human bodies do, and health problems become more commonplace.

I'm sure you may have heard that one year of a dog's life equals seven years of a human's life. Actually, by the time a dog is one year old, he has surpassed a seven-year-old child's development. Once a dog reaches adulthood, the aging of one year equals the aging that takes place in a human every five years.

The aging process is difficult to provide an exact ratio for because different breeds age at different rates. Larger dogs do not have as long a life expectancy as the smaller toy breeds. While a Great Dane may be considered elderly at age six, a Labrador Retriever will have just entered middle age at that time, and a Min Pin will not be considered a senior citizen until he is well past eight or nine years old.

The first step to caring for your older Min Pin is to realize and accept that he is growing old. This isn't always easy to do. Some symptoms of aging appear gradually and are difficult to notice. You may not see that your friend is graying around the muzzle until you look at a photograph of his earlier years and realize that he now looks far different. If you notice (and accept) the changes that will occur as your Min Pin ages and allow them to be signals specifying the need for special care, you can ensure many quality years of love and affection from your aging (but healthy) pet.

Average Age Equivalents

Dog		Human
8 months	=	13 years
1 year	=	16 years
2 years	=	24 years
3 years	=	28 years
5 years	=	36 years
7 years	=	44 years
9 years	=	52 years
11 years	=	60 years
13 years	=	68 years
15 years	=	76 years

Deafness

One of the first signs of aging is when a Min Pin who has always been responsive to your calls suddenly seems to be ignoring you. Usually, the sense of direction is the first aspect of hearing to deteriorate. Try whistling to your pet, and see if he turns in your direction. Purchasing a strong whistle to blow when you want your Min Pin's attention is oftentimes the trick to retaining good communication, as most dogs can hear high-pitched sounds long after other sounds are inaudible to them.

Eye and Vision Concerns

Older Min Pins may start to bump into things or appear generally disoriented. You may see a blue-gray tint to the eye. A canine ophthalmologist can tell you whether the diminished vision is actually due to increasing age or whether there is an underlying, possibly treatable, condition.

Dental Issues

It's extremely important to continue good dental habits with the older Min Pin. Gum and tooth decay and disease are triggers for heart problems. By keeping your Min Pin in good dental health, you will not only be making him easier to live with (by avoiding foul breath), but you will be lengthening his life expectancy.

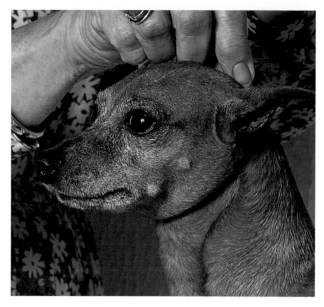

Skin Conditions

The elasticity of the skin diminishes in all mammals as they age. Cuts and bruises that once would have healed in a matter of days may take a much longer time to disappear. Tiny, wart-like bumps may appear on your Min Pin's face and other parts of the body. He may begin shedding more frequently and in greater quantities as he ages and becomes less active. None of these changes is a cause for alarm unless it seems to actually bother your Min Pin in some way. Bumps and warts that are in danger of being continuously bruised or torn during grooming or other daily activities should be removed.

Pay particular attention to your older Min Pin's eyes and teeth, as these are areas that tend to be affected by aging early on.

Tumors and cysts seem to appear overnight on the older Min Pin. Usually, these are benign cysts and fatty tumors. Because older dogs are more prone to malignancies than younger pets, you should always have any lump or bump checked by your veterinarian.

Heart Care

Early detection of heart disease in your Min Pin can prevent unnecessary pain and premature death. The earliest signal of heart failure is a low, deep, moist cough that is unaccompanied by mucus or signs of a cold. Sometimes the only treatment for heart conditions is a change of diet and exercise, but it's important that your vet give your senior Min Pin a complete checkup to rule out treatable heart problems.

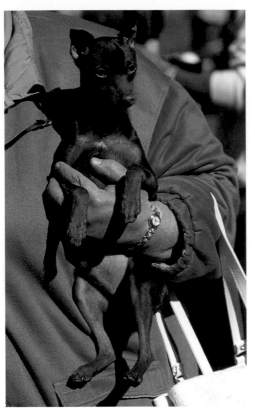

Your older Min Pin deserves some extra care and attention.

Weight

Dogs who have always been chow-hounds begging unrelentingly for additional food may suddenly suffer a loss of appetite as they pass more and more birthday landmarks. The older your Min Pin gets, the more his sense of smell and taste will weaken, so that he's likely to become less interested in food as time passes by. A decrease in weight may result from muscles becoming flabby as the senior Min Pin cuts back on both food intake and exercise.

Kidneys

You may notice that your Min Pin makes more trips to his water bowl as he gets older. An older dog may take up to two or three times more water than a younger dog. Because his kidneys do not function as well as they age, an aging canine needs extra water to maintain their efficiency. You should always mention excessive thirst to your vet.

Bowels

Your Min Pin's bowel habits will change considerably as he ages. Constipation may be brought on by a loss of muscle tone in the bowel area, by insufficient water consumption, or in older male dogs, by an enlargement of the prostate. Adding bran, cereal, liver, or fresh vegetables to your dog's diet may provide the laxative effect necessary to get things moving again. There are also some fiber diets that can be helpful.

Incontinence

As dogs of both sexes become older and muscle tone is lost from the sphincter muscle that keeps urine from escaping, even the most well-housetrained dog may have accidents. The older Min Pin usually doesn't realize that he is leaking and should never be punished for accidents that he likely couldn't control. Your veterinarian may be able to treat urinary incontinence in an older Min Pin with medication.

SAYING GOODBYE

How wonderful it would be if all our beloved pets who were ready to pass away did so in their sleep, after showing no previous signs of illness. Although this does occur at times, it doesn't always, and it will likely be up to you to decide when the time has come to say goodbye. There is no easy way to make this decision. It is human nature to want to hold on as long as possible, to keep telling yourself that "tomorrow he'll be better," until it becomes apparent that your best friend's tomorrows will be filled only with the pain and confusion of his today—and that it is within your power to ease the pain and take away the confusion. This is not a selfish decision—quite the contrary. Giving your beloved Min Pin a painless death and being with him in his final moments will likely be one of the hardest things any pet owner will ever be asked to do, but it is the last gift you can give your old friend.

Discuss euthanasia with your veterinarian as soon as your Min Pin begins to give you signals that it may soon be time to go. Some vets who generally do not make house calls will do so for the purpose of euthanasia. Most will allow or even request that the owner stay in the room with his pet until the shot has been administered and the final breaths have been taken. Don't worry about discomfort for your Min Pin during those last moments of life. Euthanasia is simply the intravenous injection of an overdose of an anesthetic drug. Quite simply, your pet will blissfully fall into one last deep sleep. His last thoughts will be of you and that you loved him enough to let him go.

ASSOCIATIONS AND ORGANIZATIONS

BREED CLUBS

American Kennel Club (AKC)
5580 Centerview Drive
Raleigh, NC 27606
Telephone: (919) 233-9767
Fax: (919) 233-3627
E-mail: info@akc.org
www.akc.org

Canadian Kennel Club (CKC)
89 Skyway Avenue, Suite 100
Etobicoke, Ontario M9W 6R4
Telephone: (416) 675-5511
Fax: (416) 675-6506
E-mail: information@ckc.ca
www.ckc.ca

Miniature Pinscher Club of America, Inc. (MPCA)
Secretary: Christine Filler
E-mail:
MPCASecretary@minpin.org
www.minpin.org

The Kennel Club
1 Clarges Street
London
W1J 8AB
Telephone: 0870 606 6750
Fax: 0207 518 1058
www.the-kennel-club.org.uk

United Kennel Club (UKC)
100 E. Kilgore Road
Kalamazoo, MI 49002-5584
Telephone: (269) 343-9020
Fax: (269) 343-7037
E-mail: pbickell@ukcdogs.com
www.ukcdogs.com

RESCUE ORGANIZATIONS AND ANIMAL WELFARE GROUPS

American Humane Association (AHA)
63 Inverness Drive East
Englewood, CO 80112
Telephone: (303) 792-9900
Fax: 792-5333
www.americanhumane.org

American Society for the Prevention of Cruelty to Animals (ASPCA)
424 E. 92nd Street
New York, NY 10128-6804
Telephone: (212) 876-7700
www.aspca.org

Royal Society for the Prevention of Cruelty to Animals (RSPCA)
Telephone: 0870 3335 999
Fax: 0870 7530 284
www.rspca.org.uk

The Humane Society of the United States (HSUS)
2100 L Street, NW
Washington DC 20037
Telephone: (202) 452-1100
www.hsus.org

SPORTS

Canine Freestyle Federation, Inc.
Membership Secretary: Brandy Clymire
E-mail:
CFFmemberinfo@aol.com
www.canine-freestyle.org

International Agility Link (IAL)
Global Administrator: Steve Drinkwater
E-mail: yunde@powerup.au
www.agilityclick.com/~ial

North American Flyball Association (NAFA)
1400 West Devon Avenue #512
Chicago, IL 60660
Telephone: (800) 318-6312
Fax: (800) 318-6318
www.flyball.org

VETERINARY RESOURCES

Academy of Veterinary Homeopathy (AVH)
P.O. Box 9280
Wilmington, DE 19809
Telephone: (866) 652-1590
Fax: (866) 652-1590
E-mail: office@TheAVH.org
www.theavh.org

American Academy of Veterinary Acupuncture (AAVA)
100 Roscommon Drive, Suite 320
Middletown, CT 06457
Telephone: (860) 635-6300
Fax: (860) 635-6400
E-mail: office@aava.org
www.aava.org

American Animal Hospital Association (AAHA)
P.O. Box 150899
Denver, CO 80215-0899
Telephone: (303) 986-2800
Fax: (303) 986-1700
E-mail: info@aahanet.org
www.aahanet.org/index.cfm

American Holistic Veterinary Medical Association (AHVMA)
2218 Old Emmorton Road
Bel Air, MD 21015
Telephone: (410) 569-0795
Fax: (410) 569-2346
E-mail: office@ahvma.org
www.ahvma.org

American Veterinary Medical Association (AVMA)
1931 North Meacham Road –
Suite 100
Schaumburg, IL 60173
Telephone: (847) 925-8070
Fax: (847) 925-1329
E-mail: avmainfo@avma.org
www.avma.org

British Veterinary Association (BVA)
7 Mansfield Street
London
W1G 9NQ
Telephone: 020 7636 6541
Fax: 020 7436 2970
E-mail: bvahq@bva.co.uk
www.bva.co.uk

MISCELLANEOUS

Association of Pet Dog Trainers (APDT)
150 Executive Center Drive Box 35
Greenville, SC 29615
Telephone: (800) PET-DOGS
Fax: (864) 331-0767
E-mail: information@apdt.com
www.apdt.com

ASSOCIATIONS AND ORGANIZATIONS

Breed Clubs

American Kennel Club (AKC)
5580 Centerview Drive
Raleigh, NC 27606
Telephone: (919) 233-9767
Fax: (919) 233-3627
E-mail: info@akc.org
www.akc.org

Canadian Kennel Club (CKC)
89 Skyway Avenue, Suite 100
Etobicoke, Ontario M9W 6R4
Telephone: (416) 675-5511
Fax: (416) 675-6506
E-mail: information@ckc.ca
www.ckc.ca

Miniature Pinscher Club of America, Inc. (MPCA)
Secretary: Christine Filler
E-mail:
MPCASecretary@minpin.org
www.minpin.org

The Kennel Club
1 Clarges Street
London
W1J 8AB
Telephone: 0870 606 6750
Fax: 0207 518 1058
www.the-kennel-club.org.uk

United Kennel Club (UKC)
100 E. Kilgore Road
Kalamazoo, MI 49002-5584
Telephone: (269) 343-9020
Fax: (269) 343-7037
E-mail: pbickell@ukcdogs.com
www.ukcdogs.com

Rescue Organizations and Animal Welfare Groups

American Humane Association (AHA)
63 Inverness Drive East
Englewood, CO 80112
Telephone: (303) 792-9900
Fax: 792-5333
www.americanhumane.org

American Society for the Prevention of Cruelty to Animals (ASPCA)
424 E. 92nd Street
New York, NY 10128-6804
Telephone: (212) 876-7700
www.aspca.org

Royal Society for the Prevention of Cruelty to Animals (RSPCA)
Telephone: 0870 3335 999
Fax: 0870 7530 284
www.rspca.org.uk

The Humane Society of the United States (HSUS)
2100 L Street, NW
Washington DC 20037
Telephone: (202) 452-1100
www.hsus.org

Sports

Canine Freestyle Federation, Inc.
Membership Secretary: Brandy Clymire
E-mail:
CFFmemberinfo@aol.com
www.canine-freestyle.org

International Agility Link (IAL)
Global Administrator: Steve Drinkwater
E-mail: yunde@powerup.au
www.agilityclick.com/~ial

North American Flyball Association (NAFA)
1400 West Devon Avenue #512
Chicago, IL 60660
Telephone: (800) 318-6312
Fax: (800) 318-6318
www.flyball.org

Veterinary Resources

Academy of Veterinary Homeopathy (AVH)
P.O. Box 9280
Wilmington, DE 19809
Telephone: (866) 652-1590
Fax: (866) 652-1590
E-mail: office@TheAVH.org
www.theavh.org

American Academy of Veterinary Acupuncture (AAVA)
100 Roscommon Drive, Suite 320
Middletown, CT 06457
Telephone: (860) 635-6300
Fax: (860) 635-6400
E-mail: office@aava.org
www.aava.org

American Animal Hospital Association (AAHA)
P.O. Box 150899
Denver, CO 80215-0899
Telephone: (303) 986-2800
Fax: (303) 986-1700
E-mail: info@aahanet.org
www.aahanet.org/index.cfm

American Holistic Veterinary Medical Association (AHVMA)
2218 Old Emmorton Road
Bel Air, MD 21015
Telephone: (410) 569-0795
Fax: (410) 569-2346
E-mail: office@ahvma.org
www.ahvma.org

American Veterinary Medical Association (AVMA)
1931 North Meacham Road –
Suite 100
Schaumburg, IL 60173
Telephone: (847) 925-8070
Fax: (847) 925-1329
E-mail: avmainfo@avma.org
www.avma.org

British Veterinary Association (BVA)
7 Mansfield Street
London
W1G 9NQ
Telephone: 020 7636 6541
Fax: 020 7436 2970
E-mail: bvahq@bva.co.uk
www.bva.co.uk

Miscellaneous

Association of Pet Dog Trainers (APDT)
150 Executive Center Drive Box 35
Greenville, SC 29615
Telephone: (800) PET-DOGS
Fax: (864) 331-0767
E-mail: information@apdt.com
www.apdt.com

ACKNOWLEDGEMENTS

Thanks to Peter Land, as always, for everything. To Rick Clark for continuing to be the world's greatest researcher. And to Ellen Trapp, DVM, for enriching my life in so many ways, not the least being her world-class care of all my pets.

Thank you guys for "being there."

ABOUT THE AUTHOR

Bobbye ("Babs") Land shares her Alabama farm home with myriad pets, including, in order of size, a horse (Story), a cow (Elizabeth), a goat (Daisy), 4 dogs (Michael, Dixie, Rose, and Halle), a cat (Merlin Monroe), a conure (Chuckles) and three dwarf hamsters. She is active in English Cocker rescue, as well as always being willing to offer a foster home to any animal in need. An avid wildlife watcher, her home is a wildlife haven. Her work resume includes not only years as a writer (with multiple books, magazine articles, and columns) but also 25 years breeding and exhibiting purebred dogs, 7 years as a veterinary assistant, and 7 years as the owner/manager of a pet grooming shop.

PHOTO CREDITS

Nylabone® Cares.

Millions of dogs of all ages, breeds, and sizes have enjoyed our world-famous chew bones—but we're not just bones! Nylabone®, the leader in responsible animal care for over 50 years®, devotes the same care and attention to our many other award-winning, high-quality innovative products. Your dog will love them — and so will you!

Toys   Treats   Chews   Crates   Grooming